Escape from Wits' End
Finding Peace Amid Peril

```
THIS BOOK IS
PROPERTY OF:
LARRY W. WYNN
```

248.8   1302
Gad   Gaddis, Todd
Escape From Wits' End: Finding Peace Amid Peril

Escape From Wits' End
FINDING PEACE AMID PERIL
Todd Gaddis

Belleville, Ontario, Canada

Escape from Wits' End
Copyright © 2005, Todd Gaddis

All Rights Reserved. No part of this publication may be reproduced, stored in a retrieval system or transmitted in any form or by any means—electronic, mechanical, photocopy, recording or any other—except for brief quotations in printed reviews, without the prior permission of the author.

All Scripture quotations, unless otherwise specified, are from *The Holy Bible, New International Version*. Copyright © 1973, 1978, 1984 International Bible Society. Used by permission of Zondervan Publishing House. All rights reserved. Scriptures marked KJV are from *The Holy Bible, King James Version*. Copyright © 1977, 1984, Thomas Nelson Inc., Publishers.

Library and Archives Canada Cataloguing in Publication

Gaddis, Todd
    Escape from wits' end : finding peace amid peril / Todd Gaddis.
Includes bibliographical references.
ISBN 1-55306-970-6

    1. Christian life. I. Title.
BT135.G28 2005   248.8'6   C2005-903629-X

Guardian Books is an imprint of *Essence Publishing,* a Christian Book Publisher dedicated to furthering the work of Christ through the written word. For more information, contact: 20 Hanna Court, Belleville, Ontario, Canada K8P 5J2.
Phone: 1-800-238-6376 • Fax: (613) 962-3055
E-mail: publishing@essencegroup.com • Internet: www.essencegroup.com

Cover Painting: Christ and the Storm;
Giorgio de Chirico, 1914; Vatican, Rome.

Table of Contents

Acknowledgements 7
Foreword 9
Introduction 11

1. Strike the Rock 17
2. Battling Depression 25
3. Confronting Confession 35
4. Beyond the Pit 43
5. It Stinks in Here 51
6. Be Still 61
7. Prison Praise 71
8. Sufficient Grace 81
9. Rusty Nails 91
10. Worthy Is the Lamb 101

Acknowledgements

I have several people to thank for helping me with this project:

Ken Hubbard for planting the seed when he preached "Escape From Wits' End Corner" at a life-changing revival meeting in the early 1980s.

The loving members and dedicated staff at First Baptist LaFayette, GA, for their encouragement and prayers.

Those special servants who took time to read the manuscript and make helpful corrections and suggestions.

My loving parents, who continue to undergird me with prayer, encouragement and help with promoting my books.

My dear daughters, for the joy they bring to my life.

My wonderful wife and best friend, who has always said, "Todd, you really need to be writing."

Most of all, I thank God, who has provided escape from wits' end more times than I can count.

Todd stopped by for a visit with Arkansas governor Mike Huckabee at a recent booksellers convention in Nashville.

Foreword

Living in a fast-paced world desensitized by the chime of incoming e-mail and the vibration of countless cellular text messages, one can easily become trapped by the quicksand of life. In *Escape from Wits' End*, Todd Gaddis offers a release from the personal "prison of fear" through trust in God and answered prayer. Understanding and confronting our weaknesses is the key to God's deliverance, and through the use of lighthearted anecdotes strengthened by relevant Scripture, Gaddis helps us brace ourselves for life's eminent storms.

Only when we stop harboring worries and begin harvesting lessons are we able to see the jubilation through the pain, the peace through the peril, and the light in the darkest corner of the world. This lesson in personal accountability brings us closer to God by urging us to accept responsibility for our own decisions while rejecting the torment of envy and resentment harbored towards the lives of others. Gaddis's masterfully written book will permanently change your perspective, and I urge you to experience the positive, life-changing power of God manifested in this great work.

Mike Huckabee, Governor
State of Arkansas

Psalm 107: 23-29

Others went out on the sea in ships; they were merchants on the mighty waters. They saw the works of the Lord, his wonderful deeds in the deep. For he spoke and stirred up tempest that lifted high the waves. They mounted up to the heavens and went down to the depths; in their peril their courage melted away. They reeled and staggered like drunken men; they were at their wits' end. Then they cried out to the Lord in their trouble, and he brought them out of their distress. He stilled the storm to a whisper; the waves of the sea were hushed.

Introduction

> *"They reeled and staggered...they were at their wits' end"*
> (Psalm 107:27).

Back in the early 1980s, I was fresh out of college and living on my own, working as a manufacturer's sales representative in southeast Michigan. Shortly after moving there, establishing residence, and unpacking, I thumbed through the local yellow pages and found a church to visit. I began attending due to guilt and habit, continued out of curiosity, and soon discovered I actually enjoyed myself.

In the spring of 1982, an evangelist came up from Tennessee to conduct a week of revival services. His messages proved life changing, especially one entitled "Escape from Wits' End Corner." I was exposed to lots of Bible teaching as a child and adolescent yet couldn't remember anything about a "wits' end." Nevertheless, a quick concordance search led me to Psalm 107.

Scholars believe this psalm was written during the period in which the Persians defeated the Babylonians, which opened the door for the Jews to return to Palestine. With Jeremiah's prediction fulfilled and Daniel's prayer answered, decades of exile would soon become a memory. With prophecy fulfilled, potential abounded.

> "The returned remnant, acutely aware of the sins of the nation that had brought about the captivity, determined to 'put first things first.' They began by building an altar for God and reinstituting the sacrifices. They began at the heart of things. They put *Calvary*, so to speak, into the center of the picture, since without a proper view of sin and redemption no nation can prosper."[1]

Then they formed the foundation of the temple, in the midst of the nation's songs and tears. Musical services established by David were heard once again. Cries of joy rang out over Jerusalem's ruined walls and bleak streets.

Psalm 107 mixes historical and future events, centered around such themes as the desert, death, imprisonment, and the perilous sea. Here, Israel is symbolized as merchant vessels on tumultuous waters. The enemy "seas" had risen at God's command, all but sinking the Jews completely. Reeling and staggering like drunkards, they were at their *"wits' end"* (Psalm 107:27). Void of courage that disappeared like an early morning fog in midday sun, they sought the Lord, and He lifted them from their distress.

This rescue represents the myriad of times throughout Scripture that God intervened to protect His people from disaster and death. To illustrate and elaborate, I have selected ten passages in which the Father delivers His children from crisis situations, one from each of the major sections of the Bible (see chart). And while a majority of these occasions take place in a historical context, doctrinal, poetic, and prophetic passages receive consideration as well.

Old Testament

Law
Genesis
Exodus
Leviticus
Numbers
Deuteronomy

History
Joshua
Judges
Ruth
I Samuel
II Samuel
I Kings
II Kings
I Chronicles
II Chronicles
Ezra
Nehemiah
Esther

Poetry
Job
Psalms
Proverbs
Ecclesiastes
Song of Solomon

Major Prophets
Isaiah
Jeremiah
Lamentations
Ezekiel
Daniel

Minor Prophets
Hosea
Joel
Amos
Obadiah
Jonah
Micah
Nahum
Habakkuk
Zephaniah
Haggai
Zechariah
Malachi

New Testament

Gospels
Matthew
Mark
Luke
John

History
Acts

Pauline Epistles
Romans
I Corinthians
II Corinthians
Galatians
Ephesians
Philippians
Colossians
I Thessalonians
II Thessalonians
I Timothy
II Timothy
Philemon

General Epistles
Hebrews
James
I Peter
II Peter
I John
II John
III John
Jude

Prophecy
Revelation

Surrounded by a magnificent orchestra, nineteenth-century showman and gifted violinist Nicolo Paganini stood playing before a capacity crowd. As he worked through a difficult piece, a string on his instrument snapped and dangled down. Beads of perspiration dotted his forehead, yet he bravely continued, improvising beautifully.

Suddenly, another string broke, horrifying the conductor—then, another. Now three limp strings dangled from Paganini's violin, yet he continued to play on the one that remained.

Upon completion of the performance, the audience jumped to its feet and, in good Italian fashion, shouted, "Bravo! Bravo!" As the applause faded, the violinist asked the people to sit down. Even though they knew there was no way they could expect an encore, they quietly took their seats.

At that point, the musician lifted his instrument for everyone to see. Signaling the conductor to begin, he turned to the crowd and bellowed, "Paganini...and one string!" He then placed the single-stringed Stradivarius under his chin and played the finale on one string, as the audience and conductor shook their heads in amazement.[2]

If you find yourself at wits' end, down to "one string," fret not. You may be in a position in which God can do His greatest work. Read on and discover vivid examples of God's power superseding situations involving the weaknesses and suffering of His followers. Don't allow pride and apathy to rob you of the escape that God has in store.

[1] John Phillips, *Exploring the Psalms: Volume Two* (Neptune, New Jersey: Loizeaux Brothers, 1988) p. 162.

[2] Charles Swindoll, *Strengthening Your Grip* (Minneapolis, Minnesota: World Wide, 1982) pp. 205-206.

Exodus 17:1-7

The whole Israelite community set out from the Desert of Sin, traveling from place to place as the LORD commanded. They camped at Rephidim, but there was no water for the people to drink. So they quarreled with Moses and said, "Give us water to drink." Moses replied, "Why do you quarrel with me? Why do you put the LORD to the test?" But the people were thirsty for water there, and they grumbled against Moses. They said, "Why did you bring us up out of Egypt to make us and our children and livestock die of thirst?" Then Moses cried out to the LORD, "What am I to do with these people? They are almost ready to stone me." The LORD answered Moses, "Walk on ahead of the people. Take with you some of the elders of Israel and take in your hand the staff with which you struck the Nile, and go. I will stand there before you by the rock at Horeb. Strike the rock, and water will come out of it for the people to drink." So Moses did this in the sight of the elders of Israel. And he called the place Massah and Meribah because the Israelites quarreled and because they tested the LORD saying, "Is the LORD among us or not?"

Strike the Rock

"What am I to do with these people?" (Exodus 17:4).

"I want a glass of water," cried the little boy, as his mother tucked him in bed and made her way down the stairs.

"You've already had a drink," she replied. "Besides, I don't want you wetting the bed."

"But Mom," he persisted, "I need a drink."

"Son, if you say another word about wanting water, you're going to get a whipping."

After a few moments of silence, the boy said, "Mom, when you come up here to spank me, would you bring a glass of water? I really am thirsty."

Likewise, as the Israelites traveled from Egypt to Sinai, they got really thirsty. Camping at Rephidim, they expected to find water, since it was believed to have been located on a wadi (a ravine that collects rain during the wet season and often forms an oasis). Unfortunately, they arrived to nothing but sand.

This isn't the first time God's people faced such a crisis. Crossing the Red Sea and arriving at Marah, they found water too bitter to drink. God instructed Moses to throw a piece of wood into the water, and when he did, it became sweet. Later, they discovered twelve springs at Elim and then enjoyed the manna and quail God provided in the Desert of Sin. By the time they reached Rephidim, however, their memories had evaporated along with the water.

Note three vital challenges that emerge from this unusual event:

First, *grasp the gravity of grumbling*. Despite God's perpetual provisions mentioned above, His people slipped into a disdainful pattern of murmuring. Here at Rephidim, they complained about the lack of water just as they had griped about its bitterness at Marah, asking Moses, "*Why did you bring us up out of Egypt to make us and our children and our livestock die of thirst?*" (Exodus 17:3). Earlier, when food was scarce, they moaned to Moses, "*If only we had died by the LORD's hand in Egypt! There we sat around pots of meat and ate all the food we wanted, but you have brought us out into this desert to starve this entire assembly to death*" (Exodus 16:3). When they found out from the spies what challenges and obstacles faced them in Canaan, the Israelites complained to Moses, Aaron, and the whole assembly, saying, "*If only we had died in Egypt! Or in this desert! Why is the LORD bringing us to this land only to let us fall by the sword?*" (Numbers 14:2-3).

Often, we treat this issue of complaining casually, as if it's a simple little sin that God expects from us. Nothing could be further from the truth. On one occasion, when the Israelites complained about their hardships, God got so angry at them that "*fire from the LORD burned among them and consumed some of the outskirts of the camp*" (Numbers 11:1). Due in part to their grumbling, the

Israelites were forced to wander in the desert for forty years while traveling to Canaan. Except for Joshua and Caleb, no Hebrew twenty years of age or older made it into the Promised Land. Their bodies fell in the desert instead (Numbers 14:26-35). Later, in the wake of more insolent activity, God killed another 15,000 with a plague (Numbers 16). When they *again* complained about a lack of food and water: "*the* LORD *sent venomous snakes among them; they bit the people and many Israelites died*" (Numbers 21:6).

Why the deadly barrage of a plague, flames, and poisonous serpents? Why would God cause a trip of a few hundred miles to take four decades and deprive so many of His people the chance to cross the Jordan? Ponder the following list to see why groaning poses such a risk.

> **Grumbling hardens the heart**—It may feel good at the time, yet often leaves a residue of guilt and regret.
>
> **Grumbling quenches the Spirit**—The Holy Spirit is very sensitive and therefore grieved (Ephesians 4:30) in an atmosphere of complaining.
>
> **Grumbling is contagious**—Our verbal discontent often breeds the same attitude in others.
>
> **Grumbling is a slap in the face of God**—By groaning and complaining, we indicate discontent with our position in life and ingratitude for what God has done for us.

The apostle Paul challenges us to "*do everything without complaining or arguing, so that you may become blameless and pure, children of God without fault in a crooked and depraved generation, in which you shine like stars"* (Philippians 2:14-15); in other words, *quit testing God and start trusting Him*, a second major essential derived from the Rephidim experience.

When the people came and complained to Moses, he said, *"Why do you put the LORD to the test?"* (Exodus 17:2) or "Based on God's deliverance and provision in the past, why would you chose to doubt Him at this stage in the journey?"

After His baptism, Jesus fasted in the wilderness for forty days. During that period of time, Satan tempted the Lord by taking Him to the highest point in the temple, saying, *"If you are the Son of God, throw yourself down. For it is written: 'He will command his angels concerning you, and they will lift you up in their hands, so that you will not strike your foot against a stone'"* (Matthew 4:6).

Jesus rebuffed Satan's temptation by saying, *"It is also written: 'Do not put the Lord your God to the test'"* (Matthew 4:7), a verse which directly refers to the central text of this chapter (see Deuteronomy 6:16).

Even while pecking away at my keyboard, in the recesses of my mind I am testing the Lord, particularly in the area of finances. My high-school-junior daughter turned sixteen a few months ago, and you know what that means—car, insurance, college, etc.

I did the responsible thing by opening up a mutual fund account for her shortly after she was born and have made regular deposits to this day. I had a handsome amount built up until the stock market fall of 2000, when it lost over half of its value. I still kick myself for not moving a portion of it into an area of less risk. But, the fact is, I didn't. So I live with myself, licking my wounds, testing the Lord.

Certainly, God has provided to this point. I've observed scores of others who've gone before me, crossed this troublesome summit, and lived to tell about it. Still, I must confess: it all seems insurmountable.

If you find yourself walking through similar spiritual minefields, meditate on Proverbs 3:5-6 along with me: "*Trust in the* LORD *with all your heart and lean not on your own understanding; in all your ways acknowledge him, and he will make your paths straight.*" Supplement that wisdom with words from the apostle Paul. "*And my God will meet all your needs according to his glorious riches in Christ Jesus*" (Philippians 4:19).

According to eighteenth-century English dramatist William Congreve, "Uncertainty and expectation are the joys of life. Security is an insipid thing."[1] Blue skies, gentle breezes, and bubbling springs will not always be present along life's twists and turns. And often, that's when the opportunity for real growth begins. This passage beckons us to stop testing God and start trusting Him instead.

As an extension of that trust, *we must follow His commands, appropriating that which He's already given us*—the final truth taken from Exodus 17:1-7 on which I want to focus. Two key concepts come to mind when considering this third challenge.

God's Presence: When Moses cried out, the Lord said, "*Take with you…the staff with which you struck the Nile, and go*" (Exodus 17:5). Here, God refers to the plague in which Moses turned the Nile River to blood with his staff (Exodus 7:20). Later, he stretched that same staff out over the Red Sea and the water began to divide (Exodus 14:16-22).

This originated at the burning bush when Moses received instructions to bring the Israelites out of Egypt and then asked, "*What if they do not believe me or listen to me and say, 'The* LORD *did not appear to you'?*" God responded by asking Moses, "*What is that in your hand?*" (Exodus 4:2). When Moses told Him it was a staff, God told him to throw it on the ground. Moses threw it on the ground and it turned into a snake. When he picked it up, it turned back into a staff. As the conversation ended, God told Moses, "*Take this staff in your hand so you can perform miraculous signs with it*" (Exodus 4:17). From that point on, a tool normally used for tending sheep became a visible reminder of God's invisible presence.

Still today, God asks related, yet different, questions of His people, especially those who find themselves at their wits' end. Who indwells you? Who desires to deliver you and, at the same time, glorify God?

Jesus sent the twelve disciples out, warning them that they would be brought before governors and kings because of Him. "*But when they arrest you, do not worry about what to say or how to say it. At that time you will be given what to say, for it will not be you speaking, but the Spirit of your Father speaking through you*" (Matthew 10:19-20).

That same Holy Spirit possesses believers today, poised to speak and serve through us, provided that as pure and willing vessels we display the following—the second key ingredient.

Our Obedience: Once receiving instructions, Moses followed them immediately and completely, thus receiving God's provision. Of course he did; didn't he always?

To answer that question, we move ahead forty years in the wilderness journey to the Desert of Zin, where again the people quarreled because no water was available. This time, God said, "*Take the staff...**Speak** to that rock...and it will pour out its water*" (Numbers 20:8, emphasis added).

Instead, Moses disobeyed by *striking* the rock twice with his staff. In the short term, God again provided, as water gushed forth. In the long term, God penalized by denying Moses the opportunity of leading the Israelites into Canaan.

Throughout time, obedience has been underestimated and too often overlooked. Take for example, Saul being rejected as Israel's king for failing to carry out God's command to attack the Amalekites and destroy everything that belonged to them. *"To obey is better than sacrifice, and to heed is better than the fat of rams"* said the prophet Samuel in his words of rebuke (I Samuel 15:22).

Helen Keller's teacher Anne Sullivan said, "I saw clearly that it was useless to try to teach her language or anything else until she learned to obey me...Obedience is the gateway through which knowledge...and love do enter the mind of a child."

The same holds for the children of God. Our obedience, coupled with His omnipotence, forms a bond against which Satan and his demons cannot prevail. When we recognize the futility of our temporal tendencies, which includes a propensity to grumble and complain, living water can flow forth like the water that gushed from the rock at Rephidim.

---

[1] John Cook, *The Book of Positive Quotations* (Minneapolis: Fairview Press, 1997) p. 388.

I Kings 19:1-9

Now Ahab told Jezebel everything Elijah had done and how he had killed all the prophets with the sword. So Jezebel sent a messenger to Elijah to say, "May the gods deal with me, be it ever so severely, if by this time tomorrow I do not make your life like that of one of them." Elijah was afraid and ran for his life. When he came to Beersheba in Judah, he left his servant there, while he himself went a day's journey into the desert. He came to a broom tree, sat down under it and prayed that he might die. "I have had enough, Lord," he said. "Take my life; I am no better than my ancestors." Then he lay down under the tree and fell asleep. All at once an angel touched him and said, "Get up and eat." He looked around, and there by his head was a cake of bread baked over hot coals, and a jar of water. He ate and drank and then lay down again. The angel of the Lord came back a second time and touched him and said, "Get up and eat, for the journey is too much for you." So he got up and ate and drank. Strengthened by that food, he traveled forty days and forty nights until he reached Horeb, the mountain of God. There he went into a cave and spent the night. And the word of the Lord came to him: "What are you doing here, Elijah?"

2

Battling Depression

> *"I have had enough, Lord...Take my life"* (I Kings 19:4).

If you don't suffer from depression, chances are someone you know does, since experts estimate that as many as forty million Americans battle the gloom.[1] Next to pain, depression is one of the major ailments that sends patients to their primary care physician.[2]

The cause of this physiological/psychological malady remains a source of contention. Many professionals in the field blame external societal issues, such as a breakdown in the family, increased materialism, media overload, and a prodigious preoccupation with "self." Others classify depression as a disease or, more specifically, a chemical imbalance. And while research reveals that those of us born since 1945 are ten times more likely to suffer from depression than those born before,[3] this "darkness of the soul" has plagued mankind for millennia, operating under assumed names and often going undiagnosed.

A prime example surfaces in the life of Elijah, the Old Testament prophet who served in ninth-century B.C. in

Israel's northern kingdom during the reigns of Ahab and his son Ahaziah.

For a while, times were good for this servant, known best for escaping death by a flaming chariot ride into heaven. God provided him with food during a severe drought. Later, spiritual awakening came to a people entangled in idol worship. Miracles abounded. And yet, in the wake of a mighty victory on Mount Carmel in which fire from the Lord fell, Elijah fled to the desert, sat under a tree and asked for death.

Why the drastic reversal? Physically, spiritually and emotionally drained, he succumbed to depression's spell, snared by the following:

The Fear Trap: Faith quickly melted into fear, once Elijah discovered that Jezebel wanted him dead.

Shoikoi Yokoi remained incarcerated for twenty-eight years, and not in your typical prison with walls, bars, and guards, but rather in a jailhouse of fear. As victory crept closer for American forces in World War II, Shoikoi served on the island of Guam. Fearing that defeat meant certain capture by the U.S., he fled to the jungle and hid in a cave. He later learned the war had ended by reading one of the thousands of leaflets dropped from American planes. Nevertheless, he feared being taken as a prisoner so much that he stayed in his cave. For over a quarter of a century, he ventured out only at night. He survived on frogs, rats, roaches, and mangoes. It was only after hunters found him that he felt safe leaving the jungle.

Unbelievable, you say—a tragic waste of life. How could this soldier have been entrenched in such anxiety?

According to Edmund Burke, "No passion so effectually robs the mind of its powers of acting and reasoning as fear."[4]

"Fear, if allowed to reign," said John M. Wilson, "would reduce us all to trembling shadows of men, for whom only death could bring release."[5]

Elijah personifies that.

The Enemy Trap: On Mount Carmel, Elijah maintained a focus on God (I Kings 18:36-37). Later, however, thoughts of the evil queen distorted his outlook and stole his joy.

Several years ago, I got an anonymous letter, severely criticizing my work at the church I served at the time. I had heard of others who received such notes, but this was a first for me. And even though this incident was isolated and unwarranted, it knocked me for a loop. My bearings of God became muddled. I launched out to discover who would dare write such stinging verbiage. I became angrier by the hour, consumed by what I perceived to be a crisis.

Similarly, Elijah's obsession with his adversary caused him to derail and, thus, lose a vision of God's work. Fear pushed the prophet to that point, a dilemma compounded by the following:

The Comparison Trap: Elijah's next mistake is revealed by his claim, "*I am no better than my ancestors*" (I Kings 19:4). Once again, rather than center his attention on God, he fretfully measured himself against people from the past.

Despite Peter's denial (see Mark 14:66-72), Jesus reinstated him during one of His post-resurrection appearances beside the Sea of Galilee. Once Christ revealed to this repentant disciple his future fate (John 21:18-19), Peter turned toward John and inquired, "Lord, *what about him?*"

Jesus replied, "*If I want him to remain alive until I return, what is that to you?* ***You must follow me.***" (John 21:21-22, emphasis added).

The comparison trap sprang on me recently as I thumbed through the newsletter from a burgeoning congregation in a nearby town. I noted that over forty people had joined their church in just one month. It took our congregation twenty months to experience the same numerical growth. Battling my envious thoughts, I heard the counsel of the Holy Spirit breaking through, "If I chose to bless that church in such a way, what is that to you?"

The Blame Trap: Elijah experienced increased misery by condemning himself for the failures of his people. Likewise, many people slip into a depressed state by blaming themselves for things over which they have no control.

I heard about a Sunday school teacher who despaired when a faithful member of her class stopped attending. For years, the teacher grappled with the possibility that she was to blame, discovering years later it was the lady's husband that kept her from attending.

Often times we invite depression into our lives by wrestling with issues over which we have no control, such as the stock market, the weather, the behavior of family members, the reaction of others to our ideas, etc. If left unchecked, we'll drift into the final pitfall, one in which Elijah found himself.

The Pity Trap: Elijah threw a pity party, justifying himself before the Lord.

> *"I have been very zealous for the* LORD *God Almighty. The Israelites have rejected your covenant, broken down your altars, and put your prophets to death with the sword. I am the only one left," he moaned, yet seven thousand faithful remained* (I Kings 19:10,18).

We tend to mire in misery and exaggerate the negative as discouragement closes in: listening to the voice of the enemy, assuming that everyone is against us, and thinking that nobody cares. The following suggestions will help build a barrier of protection against a tsunami of unhealthy emotions that often crash against us and offer an opportunity for renewal as an added bonus.

First, *take care of your physical needs*. Elijah's emotional struggles stemmed in part from physical deficiencies. Realizing the prophet's state of hunger and fatigue, an angel came twice to say, "*Get up and eat*" (I Kings 19:5,7).

Living within the confines of this present world means adhering to an inseparable connection between body and soul, the physical and spiritual. As Paul writes, "*Your body is a temple of the Holy Spirit*" (I Corinthians 6:19). Therefore, we must do everything possible to ensure that the Holy Spirit has a healthy house in which to dwell, which means sufficient rest, proper nutrition, and regular exercise are a must.

There are a lot of things I can live without, but sleep is not one of them. I have a brother-in-law who can get by on four hours a night. I need a minimum of seven and a half. If you're constantly tired, go to bed earlier. I've heard an hour before midnight is worth two after.

I may not always eat the right thing, yet I try to never overeat. Smaller portions work best for me. I am determined not to join the "growing" number of overweight Americans. I abhor the thought of becoming the stereotypical "fat" preacher. Therefore, I exercise regularly and rigorously, which keeps me fit and releases endorphins in my brain. Please don't interpret this as boasting or vanity. My intention is to encourage you. Make the first step toward subduing the blues by taking care of your temple.

Next, *consider sharing your burdens with God.* Elijah certainly did. "*I have had enough,*" he said, pouring out his soul to the Lord (I Kings 19:4).

Moses again comes to mind when considering those willing to transparently reveal their heartaches to the Lord. When Pharaoh turned up the heat and increased their workload, the Israelites fumed to their leaders, "*May the LORD look upon you and judge you! You have made us a stench to Pharaoh and his officials and have put a sword in their hand to kill us.*" Moses relayed the complaint to the Lord: "*O Lord, why have you brought trouble upon this people? Is this why you sent me? Ever since I went to Pharaoh to speak in your name, he has brought trouble upon this people, and you have not rescued your people at all*" (Exodus 5:22-23). Do you think God was offended or taken by surprise by Moses's irritation? I think not. In fact, He used this as an opportunity to re-establish His plan for the Israelites.

Most people are prone to go to family and friends when opening up about trials and hurts. And I'm certainly not nixing that as a possibility. The Bible commands us to "*mourn with those who mourn*" and to "*carry each other's burdens*" (Romans 12:15; Galatians 6:2). Yet, such venting is no substitute for going to our heavenly Father. Battling depression means offering Him our frustrations as well as our praises and thanksgiving.

Also, *anticipate a visit from God.* The first time Elijah prayed, an angel came and ministered to him. Forty days later, God Himself spoke to the prophet in a gentle whisper (I Kings 19:12).

Having preached numerous times on the life of Abraham, I marvel at the number of occasions God "visited" him. Whether by voice, vision, or personal representation, God came to call, inform, inspire and test (Genesis 12:1;12:7;13:14;15:1;17:1;18:1;22:1).

During Paul's final voyage to Rome, a storm packing hurricane force winds threatened to kill everyone aboard. Then, an angel appeared and said, *"Do not be afraid Paul...God has graciously given you the lives of all who sail with you"* (Acts 27:24). It may not be in an audible voice or by an angel; nevertheless, God still speaks.

Rick Warren advises those facing difficult circumstances: "If you are depressed, take your Bible and go to the ocean or to a lake or out in the country. Sit down and read your Bible, and get alone with God. Just let God love you and speak to you. Let Him meet your needs, and let yourself feel His presence. There is no greater antidepressant than communication and fellowship with God."[6] Even if you can't make it to the ocean, lake, or country, avail yourself to the Lord and prepare for His presence.

Finally, *shed discouragement by moving ahead with work that the Lord has for you.* God told Elijah to *"Go back the way you came...anoint Hazael king over Aram...anoint Jehu...king over Israel...and anoint Elisha...to succeed you as a prophet"* (I Kings 19:15-16).

Do you detect a fragrance of hope as Elijah receives fresh marching orders? Dejection turns to discovery. Oppression becomes opportunity and then obedience (I Kings 19:19).

When asked what to do when getting close to a nervous breakdown, psychiatrist Karl Menninger said, "Lock your house, go across the railroad tracks, find someone in need and do something for him."[7]

The same counsel fits those at all levels of discouragement. Nothing compares to the tonic of a fresh task.

Looking out windows instead of gazing into mirrors often ignites transformation.

At a time when I felt like Elijah and started springing the traps described above, an invitation came to go with a group to Russia on a short-term mission project. I took the trip and had one of the most meaningful experiences of my life. During a recent relapse, God opened the door for me to attend a Christian writers' conference. This project resulted indirectly from that opportunity.

I am a doctor but not a physician; therefore, I can't make recommendations regarding the chemical facet of what you might be struggling with. This fact remains certain, however: God wants you to experience life to its fullest, free of bouts with depression. Hopelessness and gloom must be held at bay. Join me in this march against melancholy by avoiding the traps and applying God's remedies.

---

[1] Joan-Marie Moss, NetEzShop Health Articles.

[2] Alan Clark, www.stjohns.com.

[3] *Medical Causes of Depression*, www.clinical-depression.co.uk.

[4] John Cook, *The Book of Positive Quotations* (Minneapolis: Fairview Press, 1997) p. 366.

[5] Ibid., p. 364.

[6] Rick Warren, *Answers to Life's Difficult Questions* (Wheaton, IL: Victor Books, 1985) p. 40.

[7] Raymond McHenry, *The Best of In Other Words* (Houston: Raymond McHenry, Publisher, 1996) p. 70.

Psalm 32:1-5

Blessed is he whose transgressions are forgiven, whose sins are covered. Blessed is the man whose sin the Lord does not count against him and in whose spirit is no deceit. When I kept silent, my bones wasted away through my groaning all day long. For day and night your hand was heavy upon me; my strength was sapped as in the heat of summer. Selah Then I acknowledged my sin to you and did not cover up my iniquity. I said, "I will confess my transgressions to the Lord"—and you forgave the guilt of my sin. Selah

3

Confronting Confession

"When I kept silent, my bones wasted away" (Psalm 32:3).

I heard a story about a man who sent this note to the IRS:

Dear Sirs:

Enclosed, find a check for $2,500. I've cheated on my income tax return the last two years, failing to pay the full amount. If I continue to feel guilty and miss sleep, I will send the remainder of what I owe.

Like that guy, we too often avoid making full restitution for our mistakes. Modeling Adam and Eve, we're apt to avoid reality, hide out, live in shame, and blame someone else, rather than confront and confess. Trapped in wits' end corner, we erode spiritually, and sometimes physically, ignoring the escape hatch that God provides.

Take for example David, who served as Israel's king during her golden years of unification and expansion (1000-961 B.C.). One spring, on the heels of repeated victory and sustained prosperity, this great warrior and statesman chose to stay home while his army marched off to war. It was during that break from battle that a chink in his spiritual armor became exposed—a taste for gorgeous women.

It began one evening as he climbed out of bed, took a walk on the palace roof, and spotted beautiful Bathsheba. The fact that she was married to one of his faithful soldiers did nothing to deter the king's lustful desire. Possessing great power and influence, David sent for and slept with this lovely lady, thus committing adultery. And as so often happens, he sank deeper into sin, by arranging Bathsheba's husband's death and taking her as his wife.

Not surprisingly, the unfaithful king became a miserable man. "For the best part of a year," according to John Phillips, "David put up a bold front and tried to brazen it, haunted at night, haughty by day."[1] Sin's destructive nature ate away at this gifted leader like cancer, graphically indicated by his words of anguish: *"When I kept silent, my bones wasted away"* (Psalm 32:3).

Warren Knight was one of the sharpest businessmen I ever knew. As a result of creative marketing and hard work, he transformed a mom-and-pop store into a flourishing concern that spread to large cities and numerous states. He appeared to have the model family as well—a lovely wife, three adorable children. He even taught Sunday school. Tragically, marital infidelity and financial impropriety burst his bubble and destroyed it all.

Running into Warren at a local restaurant, having not seen him for several years, I stood stunned. He looked gaunt, a shell of his former self. It wasn't long before word of his death came.

I firmly believe David was headed down a similar path of destruction when the Lord sent the prophet Nathan to confront the king with his evil actions. Challenged and chastised, David admitted guilt. He followed up by penning two of the

Confronting Confession

most powerful psalms in the Bible, Psalm 32 and Psalm 51.

Note carefully that King David's remarkable recovery began with *conviction*. He candidly acknowledged to God, *"For day and night your hand was heavy upon me"* (Psalm 32:4). A troubled conscience bore its way through his soul, like termites working their way through wood. Guilt hung over his head like a dark cloud.

Conviction first entered our world when Adam and Eve succumbed to the serpent. After eating the forbidden fruit, *"The eyes of both of them were opened, and they realized they were naked"* (Genesis 3:7). When the Israelites violated God's command and intermarried with their pagan captors, Ezra the prophet prayed, *"O my God, I am too ashamed and disgraced to lift up my face to you…because our sins are higher than our heads and our guilt has reached to the heavens"* (Ezra 9:6).

Since the ascension of Jesus and the birth of the church, the Holy Spirit serves as God's primary agent of conviction. As the Lord revealed to His disciples just hours before the crucifixion, when the Holy Spirit comes, *"He will convict the world of guilt in regard to sin and righteousness and judgment"* (John 16:8). This promise received immediate confirmation on the day of Pentecost when the Spirit invaded and Peter preached. As the people listened, *"They were cut to the heart"* (Acts 2:37).

Sir Arthur Conan Doyle, creator of Sherlock Holmes, once sent the following telegram to twelve of his highly respected friends: "Fly at once, all is discovered." Within twenty-four hours, these men of noble reputation had taken a trip out of the country.[2]

Like that of his people more than five centuries later, David's guilt "reached to the heavens." Like the Jews on the Day of Pentecost, the wayward king was "cut to the heart."

Yet, unlike Doyle's friends, he didn't flee the country. Instead, he allowed the bud of conviction to flower supernaturally into the *confession*.

Exposed and void of strength, he admitted to Nathan, "*I have sinned against the* LORD" (II Samuel 12:13)—recalling and recording later, "*Then I acknowledged my sin to you and did not cover up my iniquity. I said, 'I will confess my transgressions to the* LORD.'" (Psalm 32:5).

The word *confess* is used in various ways in the Bible. For example, we declare *belief* in Christ by confessing with our mouth that Jesus is Lord (Romans 10:10). The author of Hebrews instructs us to "*Continually offer to God a sacrifice of **praise**—the fruit of lips that confess his name*" (Hebrews 13:15, emphasis added). Like David, followers of John the Baptist came expressing their *wrongdoing*: "*Confessing their sins, they were baptized by him in the Jordan River*" (Matthew 3:6). The following gives further Scriptural insight dealing with this particular aspect of confession.

First, *God sometimes brings calamity into our lives to facilitate confession.* When Nebuchadnezzar, king of Babylon, claimed personal credit for the expansion of his empire, God drove him away from his people. For seven years, he "*ate grass like cattle. His body was drenched with the dew of heaven until his hair grew like the feathers of an eagle and his nails like the claws of a bird.*" As a result of this bizarre punishment, he "*raised his eyes toward heaven,*" a visible indication of confession and repentance. Only then, was he restored to his previous position (Daniel 4:33-34). Likewise, it took a rendezvous with a herd of pigs to break the prodigal son and bring him back to God (Luke 15:15-17).

Next, *confession must first be to God, since it is ultimately against God.* As we revisit David's words previously included, note the recipient of his admission. "*I acknowledged my sin to you...I said, 'I will confess my transgressions to the LORD'*" (Psalm 32:5, emphasis added). He composed similar words in Psalm 51:4. "*Against you, you only, have I sinned*" (emphasis added). Joseph refused an offer of illicit sex from the Potiphar's wife, saying, "*How...could I do such a wicked thing and sin against God?*" (Genesis 39:9, emphasis added). When the prodigal son, previously mentioned, came to his senses, he said to his father (a parabolic representation of God), "*I have sinned against heaven and against you*" (Luke 15:21, emphasis added).

Also, *confession is agreeing with God concerning the magnitude of our sin*. God hates sin so much that His "*eyes are too pure to look on evil*" (Habakkuk 1:13). He despises it to the degree that He could not look on as His Son bore our sin on the cross. That's what prompted Jesus' agonizing cry, "*My God, My God, why have you forsaken me?*" (Matthew 27:46).

Since God hates sin so much, it stands to reason that He wants us to feel the same way. David speaks elsewhere of a wicked person that "*flatters himself too much to detect or hate his sin*" (Psalm 36:2), a description that would fit any of us at one time or another. Battling our fleshly nature, we often vacillate concerning our position on sin. Sometimes we flee from it, on other occasions dabble in it, and, periodically, even jump in over our heads. Yet, when real conviction takes place, we view ourselves exactly the same way God does. Then, if we take the supernatural step of confession, we agree with God as to the seriousness of our sin.

David limped along in the dark for several months. But once confronted by God's messenger, he saw himself for who he really was. Making that fateful discovery, he acknowledged his wrongdoing before God, adding, "*You forgave the guilt of my sin*" (Psalm 32:5).

This encounter reveals a final principle: *Confession is a prerequisite for cleansing and forgiveness.* We can feel remorseful and guilty about our transgressions, but until we offer genuine confession to God, an obligation remains unfulfilled. The key verse that deals with this issue says, "*If we confess our sins, he is faithful and just and will forgive us our sins and purify us from all unrighteousness*" (I John 1:9).

David found this promise to be true an entire millennium before it was written, a fulfillment that brought on *comfort* from God. He moved from deterioration to celebration, claiming before God, "*You are my hiding place; you will protect me from trouble and surround me with songs of deliverance*" (Psalm 32:7).

Please note that even though the king found release from the clutches of sin, he still had to face the consequences. The son born from this forbidden tryst died just seven days after his birth (II Samuel 12:18). Describing the family dysfunction that David faced in the ensuing years goes far beyond the scope of this chapter. Nevertheless, he found forgiveness and continued to serve as one after God's "own heart" (I Samuel 13:14; Acts 13:22).

One evening while the famed evangelist D. L. Moody preached, a crime suspect on the run slipped into the anonymity of the crowd. Detective Todd B. Hall would have abandoned the chase had not the doorman, an ex-saloon keeper who knew them both, said, "If you will wait until the service is over, I will help you to get him."

Hall found a seat, sat transfixed, and later commented, "Mr. Moody was so plain in his delivery of the message that I was attracted by his earnest pleading. When through with his sermon, I was forced to decide in Christ as my Savior. The Devil said I could not be a Christian and a detective."

After the service, the criminal forgotten, Hall went straight to city hall "and told the chief of detectives and the men what I had made up my mind to do, and live the life of a Christian, and asked them for sympathy as I had enough of the tough worldly life I was living."

Arriving home later to his wife, Hall confessed unfaithfulness and begged for her forgiveness.

> We then kneeled down and asked God to help me live the Christian life and be true. When I arose to my feet, to my surprise my wife ran up to me, throwing both her arms round my neck and kissing me, said, "Nothing shall separate us. If you have made up your mind to live as a Christian, I will live it with you and take Christ as my Savior."

"Oh, what a happy family ours has been," Hall said later, "And what comfort has come to our lives...For twenty years, by the grace of God, I have been kept in that sweet life being still in the detectives' office and have been a blessing to many poor fellows who have been arrested by me, telling them what Mr. Moody told me."[3]

Why wither away at your wits' end when such freedom and forgiveness can be yours?

---

[1] John Phillips, *Exploring the Psalms*: Volume One 1-88 (Neptune, New Jersey: Loixeaux Brothers, 1988) p. 241.

[2] Raymond McHenry, *The Best of In Other Words* (Houston: Raymond McHenry Publisher, 1996) p. 123.

[3] John Pollock, Moody: *The Biography* (Chicago: Moody Press, 1963, 1983) pp. 229-230.

Jeremiah 38:6-13

So they took Jeremiah and put him into the cistern of Malkijah, the king's son, which was in the courtyard of the guard. They lowered Jeremiah by ropes into the cistern; it had no water in it, only mud, and Jeremiah sank down into the mud. But Ebed-Melech, a Cushite, an official in the royal palace, heard that they had put Jeremiah into the cistern. While the king was sitting in the Benjamin Gate, Ebed-Melech went out of the palace and said to him, "My lord the king, these men have acted wickedly in all they have done to Jeremiah the prophet. They have thrown him into a cistern, where he will starve to death when there is no longer any bread in the city." Then the king commanded Ebed-Melech the Cushite, "Take thirty men from here with you and lift Jeremiah the prophet out of the cistern before he dies." So Ebed-Melech took the men with him and went to a room under the treasury in the palace. He took some old rags and worn-out clothes from there and let them down with ropes to Jeremiah in the cistern. Ebed-Melech the Cushite said to Jeremiah, "Put these old rags and worn-out clothes under your arms to pad the ropes." Jeremiah did so, and they pulled him up with the ropes and lifted him out of the cistern. And Jeremiah remained in the courtyard of the guard.

4

Beyond the Pit

> *"They lowered Jeremiah…into the cistern…and [he] sank down into the mud"* (Jeremiah 38:6).

Once upon a time, a wealthy Texas oilman threw a coming-out party for his single, homely daughter, inviting all of the eligible bachelors from miles around. After they enjoyed a tasty barbeque lunch on the front lawn of his mansion, he took the young men around back to his Olympic-sized swimming pool, stocked with piranhas, water moccasins, and alligators. He then offered anyone who would swim the length of the pool the choice of three substantial prizes: $1,000,000 in cash, 1,000 acres of prime ranch land, or his daughter's hand in marriage.

Just as the father finished speaking, a loud splash occurred, followed by a furious bubbling and thrashing of water. Seconds later, a heavy-breathing lad sprang from the pool, his clothes tattered and torn.

Thrilled, the host congratulated the young man and asked him to choose his prize. Would he like the $1,000,000 cash? The boy shook his head no. How about the 1,000 acres? Again, the answer was no. Smiling, the father said, "Then you must want my daughter as your wife."

"No offense, sir, but I'm not interested in marrying your daughter," the young man replied.

Frustrated, the father screamed, "Then what do you want?"

The lad shot back, "I want to know the name of the guy who pushed me in the pool."

Jeremiah, who served as a prophet to Judah during the last forty years of its existence (627-586 B.C.) must have felt the same way at times. Called at age twenty, he ministered in an atmosphere of optimism and minimum opposition for nearly two decades under good King Josiah.

However, shortly after Jehoiakim took over the throne in 609 B.C., Jeremiah was threatened with death for publicly proclaiming that the temple would be destroyed (Jeremiah 26). Later, when Jeremiah's message was read before Jehoiakim, the godless ruler cut up the scroll on which it was written and threw it in the fire (Jeremiah 36:23).

Later, under king Zedekiah, Jeremiah was arrested, beaten, and imprisoned for predicting the Babylonian takeover of Judah (Jeremiah 37:15-16). Then, as conditions further deteriorated, leaders accused the prophet of treason and threw him into a mud-filled cistern and left him to die (Jeremiah 38:6). A cursory look at the life of Jeremiah, especially the cistern incident, unveils three revealing principles.

To begin with, *doing the right thing does not insulate us from the actions of mean spirited people—in fact, it might even trigger them.* God was up front with His prophet from the very beginning. "They will fight against you but will not overcome you," declared the Lord when Jeremiah was first set apart for service (Jeremiah 1:19).

When Joseph obeyed his father Jacob and went to Shechem to check on his brothers, they threw him into a cistern. Later, after he had been rescued from the pit and sold into slavery, his master's wife attempted to seduce him. Because he refused her advances, she cried rape and had him thrown into prison (Genesis 37,39).

Stephen, the first deacon mentioned in the New Testament, *"a man full of God's grace and power, did great wonders and miraculous signs among the people"* (Acts 6:8). Rather than accolades, however, his spiritual success prompted fierce opposition. After he delivered to authorities a peerless account of God's work of redemption through Abraham, Joseph, Joshua, and David (Acts 7:2-53), the people were, *"furious and gnashed their teeth at him"* (Acts 7:54). As the situation worsened, Stephen's listeners dragged him outside the city and stoned him to death.

Of course, the life of Christ demonstrates this first truth more than anyone or anything else. As God in the flesh, He never sinned. He went about doing good—preaching, teaching, healing the sick and feeding the multitudes—and in the end, he was falsely accused, given a bogus trial, and executed between two common criminals. Certainly, taking the high road doesn't exempt us from life's lows.

Next, the saga of Jeremiah *challenges us to move from comfort zone to battle zone.* Obeying God's call put the prophet in harm's way on numerous occasions, yet he marched ahead faithfully for four decades.

In the summer of 1982, thirty-three-year-old California truck driver Larry Walters took a risk of his own. Bombarded by boredom and desperate for adventure, he rigged forty-two helium-filled weather balloons to a lawn chair in San Pedro and lifted off. He brought along a pellet gun to shoot out balloons in case he rose too high—which he did. He was shocked to reach 16,000 feet rather quickly. Surprised pilots reported seeing "some guy in a lawn chair floating in the sky" to perplexed air traffic controllers. Finally, Walters had enough sense to start shooting a few balloons, which allowed him to land safely in Long Beach some forty-five minutes later.

The weird stunt earned him a Timex ad, as well as a guest appearance on the *Tonight Show*. He quit his job to deliver motivational speeches. When questioned why he pulled such a bizarre exploit, Walters generally gave the same answer: "People ask me if I had a death wish. I tell them no; it was something I had to do...I just couldn't sit there."[1]

Rescued from the Nile by Pharaoh's daughter (Exodus 2:5,6), Moses grew up in the lap of luxury. Lifelong prosperity and opportunity awaited him in the land of Egypt, yet, he decided that "he couldn't just sit there." When he grew up, he:

> *"...refused to be known as the son of Pharaoh's daughter. He chose to be mistreated along with the people of God rather that enjoy the pleasure of sin for a short time. He regarded disgrace for the sake of Christ as of greater value than the treasures of Egypt, because he was looking ahead to his reward. By faith he left Egypt, not fearing the king's anger; he persevered because he saw him who is invisible"* (Hebrews 11:24-27).

Escaping the pit involves a paradigm shift from the visible to the invisible, from the temporal to the eternal, navigating uncharted waters with a desire to please God more than man. And no one embodies this comfort zone/battle zone principle like Jesus, who willingly gave up the bliss of heaven to come to this earth to take on our sin, be forsaken by His Father, and suffer crucifixion so that we might be discover forgiveness.

Finally, *God allows us to mire in life's mud so that He*

can demonstrate His grace. I'd like to build on this Kingdom truth by listing and elaborating on this sampling of God's intervening acts on our behalf.

Rescue from peril—Earlier, I quoted the first half of a promise God made to Jeremiah during his call experience. "'*They will fight against you but will not overcome you.*'" How can this be? "'***For I am with you and will rescue you,***' declares the LORD" (Jeremiah 1:19, emphasis added). As Jeremiah descended toward demise, God kept His word and sent an Ethiopian eunuch named Ebed-Melech to organize the prophet's release. After securing permission from the king, Ebed-Melech and thirty other men made a rope of old rags and lifted Jeremiah from the pit.

The Bible teems with times in which God intervenes and rescues His children from harmful and potentially lethal situations. Daniel escaped certain execution in the lions' den when God sent an angel to shut the mouths of the dangerous beasts (Daniel 6:22). Jonah, whom we'll discuss in the next chapter, dodged a watery grave when a great fish swallowed him whole (Jonah 1:17).

Fueled by pressure from angry Jews, King Herod had James, the brother of John, killed and threw Peter in prison. As Peter lay chained and sleeping between two guards, the Lord sent again an angel to lead the disciple to freedom (Acts 12:7-10).

Shortly after the 9/11 terrorists acts, Medal of Honor recipient and dedicated Christian Desmond Doss, who now resides on Lookout Mountain in North Georgia, spoke to our congregation. Battling the Japanese on the island of Okinawa in April of 1945, Doss personally rescued seventy-five wounded soldiers from fierce battlefield conditions. Hours later, he survived a grenade attack and bullet wound to the arm. For six decades hence, Doss has testified to God's supernatural protection.

Equipping for service—So many people I know resist speaking out for Christ because they're stymied by a sense of inadequacy and a fear of knowing what to say. This has been a problem through the ages. When God called Moses at the burning bush, the reluctant shepherd resisted, claiming a lack of speaking ability. The Lord refuted that, saying, "*Who gave man his mouth? Who makes him deaf or mute? Who gives him sight or makes him blind? Is it not I, the LORD? Now go; I will help you speak and will teach you what to say*" (Exodus 4:10-12).

When Jesus sent the twelve disciples out to do ministry, He warned them that they would be brought before kings and governors on His account, adding, "*But when they arrest you, do not worry about what to say or how to say it. At that time you will be given what to say, for it will not be you speaking but the Spirit of your Father speaking through you*" (Matthew 10:19-20). Nearly seven centuries before, God challenged Jeremiah: "*Get yourself ready! Stand up and say to them whatever I command you*" (Jeremiah 1:17).

I spend a great deal of time in preparation before delivering a sermon to my congregation. Yet, more importantly, I begin my preaching by asking that God would speak His words through me, often reciting the words of David: "*May the words of my mouth and the meditation of my heart be pleasing in your sight, O LORD, my Rock and my Redeemer*" (Psalm 19:14).

Sustaining to continue—God not only rescues and equips; He sustains us by His grace—in order that we might survive and even thrive. Jeremiah could have run for the hills after being rescued from the cistern and released from prison (Jeremiah 40:4). Instead, he continued to fulfill his role. After the predicted destruction of Jerusalem in 586 B.C., the prophet experienced courteous treatment from the Babylonians and eventually went with a remnant of Jews to live out his final days in Egypt. He remained obedient to his call, even though God's people remained unrepentant.

Several years ago, I found myself in an unhappy, sometimes tumultuous, ministry situation. For a couple of years, I tried to alleviate the problem with my earthly resources. Networking with friends and sending out resumes, I'd get a nibble now and then, but nothing ever materialized. And then, unexpectedly, opportunity knocked from a church in Northwest Georgia. God worked it out, and I've been here for six years now.

As you'll read in greater detail in chapter eight, after the apostle Paul experienced an especially fulfilling and revealing experience, a thorn in the flesh—a messenger of Satan—tormented him. He pleaded with the Lord three times to relieve him of the distress, but He said to Paul, "*My grace is sufficient for you, for my power is made perfect in weakness*" (II Corinthians 12:9).

Sometimes, we mire in mud because of our own foolish actions. On other occasions, like Joseph and Jeremiah, we're pushed in the pit by mean-spirited people who have our worst interests in mind. Whatever the case, take heart. God desires to transfer us from comfort zone to battle zone, increasing our dependence on Him in the process. He allows the bad so He can demonstrate and so we'll appreciate His goodness—all the while guiding us through the wits' end maze.

---

[1] Charles R. Swindoll, *The Finishing Touch* (Dallas: Word Publishing, 1994) pp. 10-11.

Jonah 2:1-10

From inside the fish Jonah prayed to the Lord his God. He said: "In my distress I called to the Lord, and he answered me. From the depths of the grave I called for help, and you listened to my cry. You hurled me into the deep, into the very heart of the seas, and the currents swirled about me; all your waves and breakers swept over me. I said, 'I have been banished from your sight; yet I will look again toward your holy temple.' The engulfing waters threatened me, the deep surrounded me; seaweed was wrapped around my head. To the roots of the mountains I sank down; the earth beneath barred me in forever. But you brought my life up from the pit, O Lord my God. When my life was ebbing away, I remembered you, Lord, and my prayer rose to you, to your holy temple. Those who cling to worthless idols forfeit the grace that could be theirs. But I, with a song of thanksgiving, will sacrifice to you. What I have vowed I will make good. Salvation comes from the Lord."

And the Lord commanded the fish, and it vomited Jonah onto dry land.

5

It Stinks in Here

"From the depths of the grave I called for help" (Jonah 2:2).

For three days in 1987, the world held its breath while eighteen-month-old Jessica McClure remained lodged in a tiny well, just eight inches wide and twenty-two feet below ground. Left unattended for a brief time in the backyard of her aunt's Midland, Texas, day-care center, "Baby Jessica" fell into the dangerous shaft.

For fifty-eight hours, her distraught parents and an army of four hundred rescue workers worked toward a seemingly impossible rescue as an anxious nation watched alongside. The little girl sang about "Winnie the Pooh" as the crew worked to free her.

Finally, after dark on the night of October 16, 1987, prayers were answered and Jessica found freedom. "The moment we've been waiting for! She's out! She's alive," exclaimed a television anchor.[1]

After spending three days in the belly of a giant fish, a rebellious missionary found a freedom of his own on a Mediterranean beach. Jonah, who came from Gath Hepher near Nazareth, served as a Hebrew prophet during the reign of Jeroboam II (793-753 B.C.).

Jonah's story is familiar, yet bizarre. Upon receiving instructions to go east and preach against the great city of Nineveh, the administrative center of Assyria, he fled west and boarded a ship headed in the opposite direction. When a great storm arose, for which Jonah took the blame, the sailors tossed him overboard. Soon, the Lord sent the huge aquatic animal, previously mentioned, to swallow the disobedient prophet.

Days later, Jonah got another chance when he was vomited up on dry land. Receiving a second call from God, he went to Nineveh, preached, and the entire city repented and believed—even the king, who *"rose from his throne, took off his royal robes, covered himself with sackcloth and sat down in the dust"* (Jonah 3:6).

The part of this saga that draws the most attention is what Jonah does *outside* the fish. Yet, next to the conversion of thousands of unbelievers in a pagan land, the thing that inspires and instructs me the most is what takes place on the *inside*. Amidst total darkness, sloshings, rumblings, and the stench of whatever occupied the fish's stomach, Jonah voiced one of the great prayers recorded in the Bible. Note the following principles that emerge from his conversation with God.

First, as spelled out in chapter two, *perilous times present great opportunities for us to pour our hearts out to God*. This may sound like a no-brainer, yet many people allow adversity to widen, rather than bridge, the gap between themselves and the Lord. They grow bitter rather than better. Blaming God for the misfortune that befalls them, they cut off all communication with the One who loves them most.

Fortunately, Jonah saw his brush with death as a wake-up call. Floundering in the ocean currents while waves and breakers swept over him, with seaweed encircling his head, the fledgling prophet cried out to God.

King David, the central subject of chapter three, clearly represents one who willingly went to God in times of peril. Running for his life from a son who had turned against him, he lamented, "*O LORD, how many are my foes! How many rise up against me!*" (Psalm 3:1). Exhausted and depressed because of Saul's jealousy and relentless pursuit, he questioned, "*How long, O LORD? Will you forget me forever? How long will you hide your face from me? How long must I wrestle with my thoughts and every day have sorrow in my heart? How long will my enemy triumph over me?*" (Psalm 13:1-2). Victimized again by Saul's demonized treachery and hiding in a cave, David bewailed, "*I cry aloud to the LORD; I lift up my voice to the LORD for mercy. I pour out my complaint before him; before him I tell my trouble*" (Psalm 142:1-2).

If Israel's greatest earthly king, a man after God's own heart, bared the depths of his soul to his Maker, why shouldn't we? It's our unwillingness to share with Him our troubled hearts that grieves the Lord, not the act itself.

Also, *the inclusion of Scripture enriches the prayer experience.* Jonah bears witness to this claim by quoting from the psalms eight times in eight verses.[2] For instance, Jonah said, "*In my distress I called to the LORD, and he answered me. From the depths of the grave I called for help and you listened to my cry*" (Jonah 2:2).

What triggered such a plea? Consider David's agony: "*In my distress I called to the LORD; I cried to my God for help. From his temple he heard my voice; my cry came before him, into his ears*" (Psalm 18:6). Again, bear in mind these additional words from David: *"For great is your love toward me; you have delivered me from the depths of the grave"* (Psalm 86:13).

Jonah continued, *"You hurled me into the deep, into the very heart of the seas, and the currents swirled about me; and all your waves and breakers swept over me"* (Jonah 2:3). Ponder the clear connection to *"You have put me in the lowest pit, in the darkest depths"* and *"Deep calls to deep in the roar of your waterfalls; all your waves and breakers have swept over me"* (Psalm 88:6;42:7). Obviously, as a worshipping Hebrew (Jonah 1:9), Jonah was well acquainted with this poetry, much of which had been around for two to three centuries.

Including God's Word in prayer, and by that I mean praying *through* Scripture as well as reading the Bible *before* or *after*, adds supernatural buoyancy to our supplications. Obviously, this includes other situations besides those involving crises.

Years ago, while experiencing a time of spiritual stagnation, I borrowed from Jabez and asked God to *"bless me and enlarge my territory"* (I Chronicles 4:10). Soon, a short-term mission trip became available. We helped a struggling church with a building project, and I had the opportunity to preach as well.

On occasion, I've taken from David and asked God to *"Search me...and know my heart; test me and know my anxious thoughts. See if there is any offensive way in me, and lead me in the way everlasting"* (Psalm 139:23-24). It's a risky, but revealing, way to petition.

As Jack Taylor clearly states, *"Prayer and the Bible go together. Without the Bible prayer has no direction. Without prayer the Bible has no dynamic."*[3]

E.M. Bounds, author of several classic books on prayer, writes,

> The Word of God is the fulcrum upon which the lever of prayer is placed, and by which things are mightily moved. God has committed himself, his purpose, and his promise to prayer. His Word became the basis, the inspiration of our prayer, and there are circumstances under which, by importunate prayer, we may obtain an addition, or an enlargement of his promises.[4]

Jesus told his disciples in the upper room, "*If you remain in me and my words remain in you, ask whatever you wish, and it will be given you*" (John 15:7), a promise Jonah implemented nearly eight centuries before the Lord spoke the words.

Note, finally, the *vital connection between faith and prayer*. I'd like to focus on four components of faith to substantiate this connection.

First, Jonah demonstrated *confidence* that God would answer his prayer and provide rescue. Although still trapped in the big fish, he said, "*You brought my life up from the pit, O LORD my God*" (Jonah 2:6). Psalm 13 again provides illustration. As quoted, a fatigued and discouraged David moaned before the Lord. And yet, in the midst of the darkness, he focused on God's goodness. "*But I trust in your unfailing love,*" he said. "*My heart rejoices in your salvation*" (Psalm 13:5).

Having played and watched sports all my life, I firmly believe that athletes at the top of their games visualize positive results before they actually occur. Basketball players see the ball going through the net as the shot leaves their hands. Golfers picture a shot landing in or near the hole as they go through a pre-shot routine. Kickers anticipate the football going through the uprights before the ball is snapped. Likewise, wits' end escapees anticipate God's provision and relief before it actually arrives.

Note, too, that Jonah's petition involved a *return* to God. Acknowledging his banishment from the Lord's sight, he said, "*Yet I will look again toward your holy temple*" (Jonah 2:4).

In the parable of the prodigal son, the prodigal squandered his inheritance and "*longed to fill his stomach with the pods that the pigs were eating, but no one gave him anything*" (Luke 15:16). Coming to his senses, he decided to return to his father and acknowledge his sin.

Franklin Graham, CEO of the Billy Graham Evangelistic Association, sowed his share of wild oats before committing his life to Christ and rising to his top leadership position. Although living in disobedience and rebellion, he tagged along for the Lausanne (Switzerland) International Congress on World Evangelization. "Mingling with Third World Christians and recognizing the physical hardships many of them suffered moved Franklin tremendously."[5]

His belly-of-the-big-fish experience took place a few weeks later in a Jerusalem hotel room, where the twenty-two year old "threw a wadded-up pack of cigarettes in the trash, knelt by his bed, and told God, 'I want you to be Lord of my life. I am willing to give up any area that is not pleasing to you. And I'm sick and tired of being sick and tired.'"[6] Soon he returned to the straight and narrow, got married, went back to school, and announced plans to pursue vocational Christian service.

Jonah's prayer reveals *discernment,* indicated by a phrase near the conclusion of his petition: "*Those who cling to worthless idols forfeit the grace that could be theirs"* (Jonah 2:8). While soaking in a damp, dark dungeon, perhaps he recalled the fearful sailors crying out to their useless pagan gods (Jonah 1:5).

Years ago, an English clergyman paid a visit to a rich old man who was at the point of death. After giving spiritual counsel, the pastor asked if he might hold the miser's hand while they prayed together. The man declined, keeping his clenched fist beneath the bedcovers instead. Shortly thereafter, the man took his last breath, having given no assurance that he knew Jesus Christ as Savior. Later, when attendants turned down the blankets, they discovered his hand clasping the key to his safety deposit box with the rigid grip of death.[7]

For this greedy gentleman, money became the idol that snuffed out grace and possibly helped pave his way into hell. For others, it's sex, power, entertainment, career, addictions, popularity, etc. Even religion, disguised as a relationship with the Lord, can become an idol in a person's life.

Finally, Jonah demonstrates prayerful faith through his expression of *gratitude*. He proclaimed, *"I, with a song of thanksgiving, will sacrifice to you"* (Jonah 2:9).

Bummed out and bogged down, we too often go to God with concerns and requests, failing to take the time to praise and thank Him for who He is and what He's done.

When the ark was brought to Jerusalem, David penned these words: *"Give thanks to the* LORD, *call on his name; make known among the nations what he had done. Sing to him, sing praise to him; tell of all his wonderful acts"* (I Chronicles 16:8,9). A millennium later, Paul wrote, *"Give thanks in all circumstances, for this is God's will for you in Christ Jesus"* (I Thessalonians 5:18). Jonah put the apostle's words into practice hundreds of years before Paul recorded them, by expressing gratitude in the midst of his aquatic anguish.

A biblically astute cynic might ask, "If Jonah was so full of gratitude inside the fish and then so successful in Nineveh, why did he end up so angry that he wanted to die?" (see Jonah 4:3,9). The truth is, I don't know. He survived a slimy session in wits' end, yet maintained his prejudice against the Ninevites. In real life, not all stories have happy endings. Yet, as long as yours is still being written, the invitation to rise above the turmoil and live in the abundance of Christ still stands.

---

[1] www.abcnews.go.com.

[2] O.S. Hawkins, *Jonah* (Neptune, NJ: Leizeaux Brothers, 1990) p. 71.

[3] Jack R. Taylor, *Prayer: Life's Limitless Reach* (Nashville: Broadman Press, 1977) p. 111.

[4] E. M. Bounds, *Necessity of Prayer* (Grand Rapids: Baker Book House, 1976) p. 112.

[5] William A. Martin, *A Prophet With Honor* (New York: William Morrow and Company, 1991) p. 453.

[6] Ibid.

[7] Richard W. DeHaan and H.G. Bosch, *Our Daily Bread Favorites* (Grand Rapids, MI: Daybreak Books, 1967).

Mark 4:35-41

That day when evening came, he said to his disciples, "Let us go over to the other side." Leaving the crowd behind, they took him along, just as he was, in the boat. There were also other boats with him. A furious squall came up, and the waves broke over the boat, so that it was nearly swamped. Jesus was in the stern, sleeping on a cushion. The disciples woke him and said to him, "Teacher, don't you care if we drown?" He got up, rebuked the wind and said to the waves, "Quiet! Be still!" Then the wind died down and it was completely calm. He said to his disciples, "Why are you so afraid? Do you still have no faith?" They were terrified and asked each other, "Who is this? Even the wind and the waves obey him!"

6

Be Still

> *"Teacher, don't you care if we drown?"* (Mark 4:38).

A young man applied for a job as a farmhand. When the farmer asked for his qualifications, the boy answered, "I can sleep when the wind blows."

This perplexed the farmer. Nevertheless, he liked the lad, so he hired him. A few days later, the farmer and his wife awoke in the night in the midst of a violent storm. They quickly checked things out to see if all was secure. They found the shutters to the house firmly fastened and an ample supply of logs by the fireplace.

While the young man slept, the couple inspected the rest of their property. They found tools safely in storage, away from the elements. The tractor sat protected in the barn, which had been carefully locked. Even the animals were calm.

At that moment, the farmer understood the meaning of the boy's words, "I can sleep when the wind blows." Because the farmhand labored loyally and faithfully under clear skies, he was prepared when the storm rolled in. When the wind blew, he was unafraid—he could sleep in peace.[1]

On the surface, this makes for a great story. Hard work and preparation are worthy traits and usually generate satisfying rewards. Nevertheless, I find a couple of soft spots when making spiritual application. First, bad things happen to good people. You can peerlessly prepare and still get blindsided. Positive preparation provides no absolute assurance against negative infiltration. Also, this illustration implies that the young man performed totally under his own power. He is given all the credit for protecting the couple and their belongings from the elements. The central theme remains true, however. You can sleep while it storms—a reality the Lord modeled and one that and we'll explore in the pages that follow.

During one of His ministry tours of Galilee, Jesus and the disciples boarded a boat and headed toward the region of the Gerasenes, where He would eventually heal a man tormented with a legion of demons. Exhausted from His previous work, Jesus fell asleep in the stern of the craft. When a ferocious squall came up, the Lord's frightened helpers chided Him for taking a nap at such an inopportune time. He quickly calmed the storm and reproved the disciples for their meltdown of faith. Two major Kingdom principles emerge from this classic miracle of nature.

Expect storms. Just like this tempest popped up menacingly and unexpectedly on the Sea of Galilee 2,000 years ago, unwelcome trials and tribulations reach up and grab us today. The Bible says, *"Consider it pure joy, my brothers, whenever [not, if ever] you face trials of many kinds"* (James 1:2, emphasis added).

As I type these words, category four hurricane Ivan is about to make landfall on the central Gulf Coast. One such storm a season is horrendous, but what about three in the same general vicinity within five weeks? First, hurricane Charley made landfall on the gulf side of Florida. Three weeks later, Frances hit shore on the Atlantic coast. Combined, the first two storms caused several dozen deaths and over twenty billion dollars in property damage. Add to that Ivan the Terrible and, oh yeah, tropical storm Jeanne, which looms twenty-five miles southeast of San Juan, Puerto Rico...you get the picture.[2] Those in the path of these meteorological monsters could sure relate to this autobiographical account from the apostle Paul:

Five times I received from the Jews the forty lashes minus one. Three times I was beaten with rods, once I was stoned, three times I was shipwrecked, I spent a night and a day in the open sea, I have been constantly on the move. I have been in danger from rivers, in danger from bandits, in danger from my own countrymen, in danger from Gentiles; in danger in the city, in danger in the country, in danger at sea; and in danger from false brothers. I have labored and toiled and have often gone without sleep; I have known hunger and thirst and have often gone without food; I have been cold and naked (II Corinthians 11:24-27).

This sounds like baseball Hall of Fame catcher Gary Carter, a Christian and member of the 1986 World Series champion New York Mets, who admitted:

Except for a few games here and there, the only time I wasn't playing hurt was when I was too hurt to play. I had four operations on my right knee during my active playing days, and another operation on both knees in October 1992, immediately following my retirement. I had two broken thumbs, three broken ribs, ligament tears in both ankles, a busted-up toe, chronic pain in my right knee, and a nagging back ailment that got worse with age. And that's not counting the hundreds of foul tips that rifled into me, bruising almost every inch of my body at one time or another.[3]

Whether it's physical, mental, spiritual, or emotional in nature, getting injured and having to play hurt is part of life. Attempting to totally shield oneself from trouble is like trying to exist without breathing. Jesus said in the Sermon on the Mount, *"Each day has enough trouble of its own"* (Matthew 6:34).

Take, for example, Tyler, a smart kid from a solid family, working through his third year of medical school at a large state university in the South. Lightning struck when a knot on his collarbone led to a diagnosis of Hodgkin's disease. With his education interrupted, he is undergoing a series of chemotherapy treatments. Fortunately, statistics indicate a 95 percent recovery rate—the outlook is good.

Consider also hard-working and well-respected Alex, who discovered that his wife of twenty-six years was having an affair. He didn't see it coming. They're separated and haven't spoken in several months—the outlook isn't good.

I could write volumes on these sorts of issues. The list grows daily. We live in a fallen, sin-soaked world. The question is, "What are you going to do when the storm hits?"—an inquiry that points smoothly toward the second half of this chapter.

Experience rest. The fact that Jesus falls asleep in the stern of the boat symbolizes the attainable possibility of experiencing serenity—even in the worst of times. He preached what He practiced by proclaiming to the Galilean crowd,

> *"Come to me, all you who are weary and burdened, and I will give you rest. Take my yoke upon you and learn from me, for I am gentle and humble in heart, and you will find rest for your souls. For my yoke is easy and my burden is light"* (Matthew 11:28-30).

What can this incident involving Christ calming the sea teach us about experiencing rest?

First, *immediate relief is a possibility.* Once Jesus made His command, the wind stopped and the waves disappeared. From a human standpoint, this was the best-case scenario. In fact, most of the miracles that take place in the Bible represent an immediate response from God.

Once learning of Tyler's condition mentioned above, we gathered around him in a service and prayed that God would remove the disease. Although that particular prayer wasn't answered at once, it could have been. And though I'm skeptical of much of the healing that takes place on religious television, I know in my heart it can happen—I've seen it!

John G. Paton, a missionary to the New Hebrides Islands, gives this inspiring account of God's immediate provision. Violent natives surrounded the mission station one night, intending to burn the Patons out and kill them. John and his wife prayed that God would deliver them. The next morning, they discovered the attackers had disappeared.

A year later, the tribe's chief became a Christian. When asked what had kept him from burning and killing, the chief responded, "Who were all those men you had with you there?"

"There were no men there, just my wife and me," said Paton.

The chief replied that he had seen hundreds of big men in shining garments with drawn swords in hand. Paton then realized that God sent angels to protect them.[4]

For obvious reasons, God chose to answer the Patons immediately. He's done the same for me on numerous occasions. At other times, however, He chooses to delay. If you find yourself in the midst of turmoil, even though you've sought release, also consider that *a delay may prove more valuable than a swift yes*. Scripture says, "*For my thoughts are not your thoughts, neither are your ways my ways, declares the* LORD," (Isaiah 55:8)—a truth that I believe encompasses God's timing and the way He answers our pleas.

What happens to children who get everything they want as soon as they want it? They become spoiled and selfish, often anguishing as adults because of instant gratification in adolescence. The same principle applies to God's children. He often withholds in order for us to develop an intimate relationship with Him and a deeper appreciation for His provisions.

Consider another occasion, one in which Jesus was not present, when the disciples once again sailed on the Sea of Galilee (Matthew 14:22-36). When evening came, as the Lord prayed on a mountain, dangerous waves and wind buffeted the boat. Yet, Jesus waited until the fourth watch of the night (3:00 A.M. or later), before coming to the rescue. I believe the Lord allowed the disciples to experience extended tribulation in order to test and increase their faith. Faith is like a muscle. Unused, it becomes flabby, often atrophying. The Bible says that, "*Faith is being sure of what we hope for and certain of what we do not see...And without faith it is impossible to please God*" (Hebrews 11:1,6). Also, without faith, it is impossible to experience true rest.

Finally, *recognize the connection between God's Word and rest.* Once Jesus woke from His nap, He *"rebuked the wind and said to the waves, 'Quiet! Be still!' Then the wind died down and it was completely calm"* (Mark 4:39). It should come as no surprise that the One who created the wind and seas (Colossians 1:16) would also have the power to control them.

As Jack Taylor states, "All life is derived from His Word and all life is sustained by His Word."[5] For example, Psalm 107 records a pitiful description of those who rebelled against God, spurning His counsel: *"Some sat in darkness and the deepest gloom, prisoners suffering in iron chains."* Others *"stumbled and there was no one to help"* (Psalm 107:10,12). But they cried to the Lord and *"He sent forth his word and healed them"* (Psalm 107:20).

In my book *The Compliments of Christ*, I devoted an entire chapter to a Roman centurion who asked Jesus to cure his paralyzed servant. Recognizing the Lord's authority and exuding great trust, the officer said, ***"Just say the word, and my servant will be healed"*** (Matthew 8:8, emphasis added). Complimenting the centurion's faith and disregarding the fact that the sick man was not present, Jesus spoke a message of healing affirmation, and the man recovered at that very hour.

A woman who had experienced an unusually heavy amount of suffering asked her pastor, "*When* am I going to get out of these troubles?"

He responded intuitively, "You should have asked, '*What* am I going to get out of these troubles?'" Another, more seasoned, saint, recognizing the value of affliction, wisely declared, "I could have done without many *pleasures,* but I could not have spared *one sorrow* that God allowed to come into my life!"[6]

Although terrified at the time, the tenderfoot disciples that accompanied Jesus in the boat would look back on this experience as a valuable lesson learned. Soon, they'd tackle the task of spreading the gospel around the world of their day. Eventually, and for all eternity, their names (with *Matthias* replacing *Judas*) will appear on the twelve foundations of the wall of the Holy City, the New Jerusalem (Revelation 21:14). God used multiple difficulties, such as the storms that popped on the sea two millennia ago, to train them for the mission at hand and to help qualify them for the honor that will be theirs.

Likewise, God allows us to face the blows of times to mold us into the image of His Son and prepare us for the bliss of eternity. And if we're receptive and attentive, His Word augments the process through His instructive, redeeming, peace-producing power.

---

[1] Ivan hit land in and around Gulf Shores, AL, packing 130 mile per hour winds. It became the deadliest hurricane to hit the U.S. since Floyd in 1999, killing thirty-eight. After pulverizing the coastal areas, it soaked a swath from Ohio to Georgia.

Tropical storm Jeanne became hurricane Jeanne, killing over 1,000 in Haiti before slamming the U.S. Atlantic coast just south of Fort Pierce, FL. Florida became the first state to experience four hurricanes in a season since Texas in 1986.

[2] *www.storybin.com.*

[3] Gary Carter, *The Gamer* (Dallas: Word Publishing, 1993) p. 235.

[4] Billy Graham, *Angels* (Waco, TX: Word Books, 1975) pp. 16-17.

[5] Jack R. Taylor, *The Word of God with Power* (Nashville: Broadman & Holman, 1993) p. 65.

[6] Richard W. DeHaan and H.G. Bosch, *Our Daily Bread Favorites* (Grand Rapids, MI: Daybreak Books, 1967).

Acts 16:22-34

The crowd joined in the attack against Paul and Silas, and the magistrates ordered them to be stripped and beaten. After they had been severely flogged, they were thrown into prison, and the jailer was commanded to guard them carefully. Upon receiving such orders, he put them in the inner cell and fastened their feet in the stocks. About midnight Paul and Silas were praying and singing hymns to God, and the other prisoners were listening to them. Suddenly there was such a violent earthquake that the foundations of the prison were shaken. At once all the prison doors flew open, and everybody's chains came loose. The jailer woke up, and when he saw the prison doors open, he drew his sword and was about to kill himself because he thought the prisoners had escaped. But Paul shouted, "Don't harm yourself! We are all here!" The jailer called for lights, rushed in and fell trembling before Paul and Silas. He then brought them out and asked, "Sirs, what must I do to be saved?" They replied, "Believe in the Lord Jesus, and you will be saved—you and your household." Then they spoke the word of the Lord to him and to all the others in his house. At that hour of the night the jailer took them and washed their wounds; then immediately he and all his family were baptized. The jailer brought them into his house and set a meal before them; he was filled with joy because he had come to believe in God—he and his whole family.

7

Prison Praise

> *"Sirs, what must I do to be saved?"*
> (Acts 16:30).

The Shawshank Redemption, a movie based on a Stephen King novella, was one of the top movies made in the 1990s and is arguably the best prison film ever. The story begins in 1947, when Andy Dufresne, a banker played by Tim Robbins, is wrongfully convicted for murdering his adulterous wife and her lover. He then receives, and begins serving, a life sentence.

While tolerating prison life, he befriends fellow inmate Ellis "Red" Redding, portrayed by Morgan Freeman. For over two hours, the viewer sees Andy quietly going about his business—assisting the guards with tax returns, upgrading the library, helping prisoners earn their GEDs, and keeping the corrupt warden's finances. What we don't see is Andy boring a tunnel through several feet of solid wall with a rock hammer, which he keeps hidden in his Bible. Year after year, he digs and deposits the debris, a handful at a time, down his pant leg, onto the courtyard.

Finally, after two decades, he breaks through. And when the night of the big escape comes, he crawls to freedom through 500 yards of stinking sewer pipe. As the show ends, Andy, while working on a sailboat on the Mexican Pacific coast, is joined by his paroled pal Red.

As we advance from the Gospels into Acts, Paul and coworker Silas find themselves in a similar situation to that of Andy Dufresne—unjustly punished, serving time in jail.

While in the midst of extensive missionary work in Macedonia, the famed apostle and his associate encountered a demon-possessed, fortune-telling slave girl, who made her masters rich by predicting the future. For days, she followed God's servants around shouting, *"These men are...telling you the way to be saved"* (Acts 16:17). Paul became so burdened by it all that he directly addressed the evil spirit, *"In the name of Jesus Christ I command you to come out of her!"* (Acts 16:18). Immediately, the spirit left her.

This created, for Paul and Silas:

Problems—What helped the girl, hurt her owners. In fact, when she found freedom from her vexation, they seethed with *indignation*. Because their source of income disappeared along with the evil spirit, they dragged the missionaries before the magistrates and said, *"These men are Jews, and are throwing our city into an uproar by advocating customs unlawful for us Romans to accept or practice"* (Acts 16:20-21). Fueled by latent anti-Semitism and racial pride, a mob joined in the attack.

Jackie Robinson, the grandson of a slave, overcame a myriad of obstacles and became a baseball Hall of Famer. In 1947, Robinson became the first black player to break into the major leagues, a move replete with controversy. "Pitchers often threw the ball directly at Robinson, base runners tried to spike him, and he was subjected to a steady stream of racial insults. He received hate mail, death threats, and even warnings that his baby would be kidnapped."[1]

Bigotry of a similar, yet different, sort triggered the trepidation and false accusations that eventually led to Paul and Silas's incarceration. As the situation escalated, officials ordered them stripped and whipped. *"After they had been severely flogged, they were thrown into prison, and the jailer was commanded to guard them carefully. Upon receiving such orders, he put them in the inner cell and fastened their feet in the stocks"* (Acts 16:23-24).

Scripture contains numerous examples of faithful, innocent servants being thrown into prison. As previously mentioned, Joseph spent years behind bars after his boss's wife accused him of rape (Genesis 39:16-20). *"Jeremiah was put into a vaulted cell in a dungeon"* (Jeremiah 37:16) for proclaiming God-given prophetic words (see chapter four). John the Baptist went to prison for exposing Herod's illegal and immoral taking of his brother's wife (Matthew 14:3-4). In an effort to placate unbelieving Jews, Herod put Peter in jail and had him carefully guarded by sixteen soldiers (Acts 12:4).

Corrie ten Boom is widely considered one of the twentieth century's true heroes of the faith. She was born into a devoted Christian family in Haarlam, Holland. During the Second World War, the ten Boom home became a refuge for those hunted by the Nazis, many among them being Jews. They kept out of sight behind a false wall in Corrie's bedroom.

In early 1944, the family was betrayed, and the Gestapo raided their house, resulting in their imprisonment. The father died just ten days into his incarceration. Corrie and her sister Betsie spent nearly a year in three different prisons, the last being the infamous Ravensbruck concentration camp near Berlin. Betsie died in Ravensbruck, but Corrie survived and was eventually liberated.

Later, she embarked upon a global ministry that took her into more than sixty countries. Her book, *The Hiding Place*, became a bestseller and major motion picture. She died on her ninety-first birthday in April 1983.

Like the ten Booms, Paul and Silas kept the faith during their prison experience, as indicated by their:

Praise—Rather than complain or remain in lethargic silence, the missionary pair took the high road. At a time when the two could have been reeling over unjust treatment, they prayed and sang hymns to God instead.

During the reign of Jehoshaphat (873-849 B.C.), Judah came under siege by a coalition of enemy forces.

> *The good King prayed and the Spirit spoke through a Levite named Jahaziel: "You will not have to fight this battle. Take up your positions; stand firm and see the deliverance the Lord will give you, O Judah and Jerusalem. Do not be afraid; do not be discouraged. Go out and face them tomorrow, and the Lord will be with you"* (II Chronicles 20:17).

Rather than attacking the enemy with knives and spears, a selected group of Judah's army sang to the Lord and praised Him for the splendor of His holiness. In the end, God's people won the battle when the opposition turned on and destroyed one another.

When Corrie and Betsie ten Boom arrived at Ravensbruck, authorities led them to quarters with no sides, a canvas roof, and straw-covered floors. They sat down to a shocking discovery of "Lice! The straw was literally alive with them. We stood for a while, clutching blankets and pillowcases well away from the infested ground. But at last we spread our blankets over the squirming straw and sat on them."[2] Later, a commotion broke out and SS guards forced prisoners out to open ground, where they would spend the night. As the blanket-covered sisters stretched out in the elements, Betsie sang in a sweet soprano and others joined in, "The night is dark and I am far from home...lead Thou me on."[3]

Betsie modeled a basic Kingdom principle, similar to a point I made in regard to Jonah in chapter five: *Even though we may not "feel like" taking advantage of them, times of tribulation open the door to great praise opportunities.* Recall Jonah from chapter five. Trapped in the stomach of a giant fish, he sang, "*I, with a song of thanksgiving, will sacrifice to you*" (Jonah 2:9). Then the Lord caused the big fish to release Jonah on dry land.

Whether through word or song, praise to God packs powerful potential. This exercise, which currently engrosses celestial angels and will involve heavenly citizens throughout eternity, serves a variety of purposes in time, for today. Although entire books exist on this untapped subject, let me touch on a few key issues.

First, *praise paves the access road to God*. The psalmist instructs us to "*Enter his gates with thanksgiving and his courts with praise*" (Psalm 100:4). Far too often, we try to sneak into God's courts by climbing over a fence or lunge into His presence by crashing through a wall.

Focus upon another Kingdom principle: *While God is omnipresent, that is, present in all places at all times, He is not everywhere manifested.* His Spirit is too often shunned or quenched. However, He's always in His element in a praise-charged atmosphere. Praise is where He lives. As David writes, *"But thou art holy, O thou that inhabitest the praises of Israel"* (Psalm 22:3, KJV) As Jack Taylor sums it up, "That worship experience which is begun or prefaced with praise will consummate in glad fellowship with Holy God who not only dwells in but is approached by the praises of His people."[4]

Note, also, that *praise helps protect us from our enemy*. The devil and his demons despise our praising God. Why? As Lucifer and his band of fallen angels, they had experienced bliss for themselves. Tragically, they lost it and were cast from heaven due to pride and rebellion (see Isaiah 14). Taylor states, "Their ranks are broken. Like metal scratching glass is the sound of praises to them...Their influence is neutralized and their lies are exposed by praise. Praise puts them to flight."[5]

Closely aligned to the preceding point is the fact that, *praise facilitates divine deliverance*. Plagued by criticism and physical sufferings, Jeremiah said, *"Sing to the* LORD! *Give praise to the* LORD! **He rescues the life of the needy from the hands of the wicked"** (Jeremiah 20:13, emphasis added). This promise became reality to the prophet on more than one occasion (see chapter four).

Likewise, this potentiality transformed into actuality as Paul and Silas sang, preparing the seedbed for God's:

Provision—Just like the Lord protected His people and prophets previously mentioned, He provided escape for Paul and Silas as well. While the missionary pair sang, a violent earthquake hit, one that burst open the jail doors and broke the shackles that bound the prisoners.

This is not the first time God used such a catastrophic event to assist His servants. Allow me to revisit an incident

I mentioned in the first chapter, the one in which several thousand Jews were killed because they complained. The tragedy began as the Israelites traveled from Sinai toward the Promised Land. Three insolent men incited 250 well-known community leaders to join them in an uprising against Moses' leadership. Because these men rebelled,

> *the earth opened its mouth and swallowed them, with their households and all Korah's men and all their possessions. They went down alive into the grave, with everything they owned; the earth closed over them, and they perished and were gone from the community* (Numbers 16:32-33).

Just like the splitting ground spared Moses further threats from this band of troublemakers, an earthquake provided liberation for Paul and Silas. Yet as heartening as their temporal release surely was, it pales in comparison to the eternal emancipation experienced by the guard. The Bible says that, *"The jailer woke up, and when he saw the prison doors open, he drew his sword and was about to kill himself because he thought the prisoners had escaped"* (Acts 16:27).

Paul immediately intervened, informing him that they were still there. The jailer then trembled before the missionaries, asking, *"'Sirs, what must I do to be saved?' They replied, 'Believe in the Lord Jesus, and you will be saved—you and your household'"* (Acts 16:30-31). After hearing the gospel, the jailer and his family were converted.

Focus on three results of this conversion experience. First, he and his entire family were *baptized*. In an act of obedience, they wanted to show outward evidence of an inward change that had taken place in their lives. Over the years, I've encountered many believers who want to join our church but resist, due to fear or rebellion. Others who "made decisions" were baptized as children but didn't become true believers until years later. This doesn't qualify as scriptural baptism. The order must be correct—salvation, then baptism.

Notice, also, the jailer's demonstration of *hospitality*, *à la* Andy Griffith and Aunt Bea: he brought the two missionaries into his home and fed them. Paul urged the Romans to *"practice hospitality"* (Romans 12:13). Peter concurred by writing, *"Offer hospitality to one another without grumbling"* (I Peter 4:9). The author of Hebrews said, *"Do not forget to entertain strangers, for by so doing some people have entertained angels without knowing it"* (Hebrews 13:2).

Finally, we find proof that praise is contagious. Scripture says the jailer *"was filled with joy because he had come to believe in God—he and his whole family"* (Acts 16:34, emphasis added). According to research, the number one factor that draws unbelievers into church is the demonstration of joy in the lives of Christians.

Praise provided and prevailed. The jailer told Paul, *"The magistrates have ordered that you and Silas be released. Now you can leave. Go in peace"* (Acts 16:36). This same freedom and peace remains available two millennia later. Experience what only God can give, and *go in peace!*

---

[1] *www.biography.com*.

[2] Corrie ten Boom with John and Elizabeth Sherrill, *The Hiding Place* (Carmel, NY: Guideposts Associates, Inc., 1971) p. 173.

[3] Ibid., p. 174.

[4] Jack R. Taylor, *The Hallelujah Factor* (Nashville: Broadman Press, 1983) p. 30.

[5] Ibid., p. 33.

II Corinthians 12:7-10

To keep me from becoming conceited because of these surpassingly great revelations, there was given me a thorn in my flesh, a messenger of Satan, to torment me. Three times I pleaded with the Lord to take it away from me. But he said to me, "My grace is sufficient for you, for my power is made perfect in weakness." Therefore I will boast all the more gladly about my weaknesses, so that Christ's power may rest on me. That is why, for Christ's sake, I delight in weaknesses, in insults, in hardships, in persecutions, in difficulties. For when I am weak, then I am strong.

8

Sufficient Grace

> *"Three times I pleaded with the Lord
> to take it away from me"*
> (I Corinthians 12:8).

We're used to hearing about people burdened with physical pain, so you can imagine my shock when reading about a little girl who struggles with a lack of it. When most of us are hurt, our body sounds an alarm. But such feeling is foreign to Ashlyn Blocker of Blackshear, Georgia, who suffers from what's called "congenital insensitivity to pain with anhidrosis" (or CIPA), a rare genetic disorder that affects nerve endings.

Family photos show Ashlyn with a swollen lip that she bit and a burned hand that she placed on a hot appliance. She's even knocked out teeth on numerous occasions. Dr. Felicia Axelrod of NYU Medical Center said, "One would think that a world without pain might be a blessing, but pain has been given to us to protect us"[1]— a truth Paul discovered and passed along to the church at Corinth.

Fourteen years before this apostle from Tarsus wrote his second epistle to the Corinthians, Paul experienced a bizarre journey into the third heaven. Recording the details in the third person, he stated, "*And I know that this man—whether in the body or apart from the body I do not know, but God knows—was caught up to paradise. He heard inexpressible things, things that man is not permitted to tell*" (II Corinthians 12:3-4).

Although some scholars think Paul is referring to the time he was stoned in Lystra (Acts 4:19), the incident remains a mystery. And because of the potential headlines that goes along with such a privileged revelation, Paul received a thorn in the flesh, a messenger of Satan, to counter any conceit that might develop.

Like the vision itself, the specifics of this thorn in the flesh stay unknown. The consensus says that the missionary suffered from a recurrent physical condition—perhaps headaches, eye trouble, epilepsy, or even malaria. We don't know for sure. What can be clearly stated is that Paul drifted from paradise to his wits' end, repeatedly begging God for relief. Though the Lord chose not to remove the thorn, He did provide the necessary grace for Paul to survive and thrive during the pain. Several spiritual truths emerge from this episode.

First, understand that *conceit sabotages Christian growth*. Paul received "*surpassingly great revelations*" (II Corinthians 12:7), an experience that packed potential arrogance and pride.

Vince Lombardi, the legendary coach of the Green Bay Packers, became accustomed to fans asking for his autograph. Once, while dining in public, he spotted a child approaching his table. Lombardi quickly grabbed a menu and scribbled his name. When the youngster arrived at the famed coach's table, Lombardi handed him the autographed menu. "I don't need a menu," said the child, "I just need to borrow your ketchup."[2]

Most of us could use an experience like that on occasion to remind us that God is God and we're not. Conceit fills us up with ourselves to the point that little room remains for the Holy Spirit and others.

After the flood, the people, who all spoke the same language, began a massive construction project. They boasted, "*Come, let us build ourselves a city, with a tower that reaches to the heavens, **so that we may make a name for ourselves** and not be scattered over the face of the whole earth*" (Genesis 11:4, emphasis added). Realizing their self-centered motive, God broke up the party by confusing their language to the point that they could not understand one another.

In the prime of a reign that spanned five decades, King Nebuchadnezzar of Babylon proclaimed from the roof of his palace, "*Is not this the great Babylon **I have built** as the royal residence, by **my power and for the glory of my majesty?**"* (Daniel 4:30, emphasis added). With those words fresh on the king's lips, God stripped him of his authority and drove him away from his subjects. While in exile, he ate like a cow, grew hair like the feathers of an eagle and nails like a bird's claws. It was only after he chose to honor and glorify God instead of himself that Nebuchadnezzar's position was restored.

Someone quipped, "A man wrapped up in himself is a pretty small bundle."[3] Another said that "A conceited man is like a man up in a balloon: everybody looks small to him and he looks small to everybody."[4] Solomon penned, "*Pride goes before destruction, a haughty spirit before a fall*" (Proverbs 16:18). Paul wrote, "*Do not think of yourself *more highly than you ought, but rather think of yourself with sober judgment, in accordance with the measure of faith God has given you*" (Romans 12:3). To quote John Ruskin, "Conceit may puff a man up, but never prop him up."[5] Paul's battle with the thorn reveals the Lord's distaste for conceit.

Next, it teaches us that *God allows crooked sticks to keep us straight.* Shortly after Paul found salvation and was blinded on the road to Damascus, God sent a disciple named Ananias to restore his sight (Acts 9:12). When a deadly storm arose during that same apostle's voyage to Rome, God sent an angel to relay hope and encouragement. Yet, in the text at hand, a messenger of Satan accomplishes a noble purpose.

The Jews typically attributed severe and painful diseases to the devil. And while Satan is ultimately the primary source of all physical suffering, I believe God permitted and even orchestrated this trial. Satan would have loved for Paul to become egocentric, so the apostle would focus on self and seek his own glory.

God allows these thorns, which invade in the form of afflictions, situations, and even people, so we'll learn to depend wholly and solely on Him. It's not a matter of punishment for something bad but rather of prompting and positioning for something better. Take Job, for example, whom God suggested to Satan as a prime case study for affliction (Job 2:3). While this righteous man suffered tremendous pain and loss for a time, he emerged better than ever (Job 42:12).

When you get down to it, the Old Testament is an ongoing record of God using crooked sticks to lead His people and accomplish His purposes. He hardened

Pharaoh's heart so the Hebrews would flee Egypt and journey to the Promised Land. The Philistines performed the role of Israel's principal enemy from 1200-1000 B.C. Although they are typically remembered in a negative sense, they actually served as a culturally civilizing influence on the Jews. More significantly, however, "The external opposition of the Philistines brought the bickering and rival tribes of Israel together and forged them into a nation as nothing else could have done."[6] The Babylonians, Assyrians, Persians, Greeks, and others performed similar functions over the centuries as the obedience of God's people fluctuated and the time of Christ's first coming neared.

I've lost my job involuntarily only once in life, an event that took place in early 1990. I was working as a field representative in the northeast, enduring astronomical sales expectations and unreasonable management. The crux of the matter, however, was the spiritual battle taking place. Like Jonah in chapter five, I was resisting God and His plan for my life. Although I'd trained for vocational ministry, I was trying to go backward instead of forward. Once that big fish spit me out on shore, however, a church called me, and I have preached and been a pastor ever since. The Lord took a potentially devastating situation and used it to get me where I needed to be.

God wants to establish and authenticate us as His special servants. On occasion, this means receiving blessings that come pouring out of heaven. At other times, He permits trials and temptations to burn away any present and potential impurities. Solomon said, *"Remove the dross from the silver, and out comes material for the silversmith"* (Proverbs 25:4). Centuries later, Paul learned that unwanted, seemingly unpleasant circumstances form us into superior material in the hands of our Divine Silversmith.

Finally, this passage of Scripture underscores the Kingdom axiom that *we can and should delight in our weaknesses*. From a worldly point of view, this statement sounds absurd. Aren't we to ignore our frailties and inflate our strengths? After all, isn't it all about gaining and flaunting power?

Paul learned otherwise. He asked three times that the thorn be removed, but the Lord had another idea, answering, "*My grace is sufficient for you, for my power is made perfect in weakness*" (II Corinthians 12:9). Grasp the scope of this promise from Jesus.

First, *God's grace is sufficient.* Given His omniscience, God saw this as a grand opportunity to expand Paul's capacity to believe, by allowing the affliction to remain. We risk becoming spiritually soft and tend to ignore God when positive answers repeatedly come clearly and swiftly.

Am I wise to give my daughters everything they want or say yes to their every request? Should I rush in and bail them out every time they run into difficulty? The obvious answer is no, and the same principle applies between God and His children. He didn't send His Son to die like a criminal simply to keep us out of hell. God wants to develop a love relationship with us, modeled after the one that exists between Jesus and Him. Trials and tribulation create fertile soil for such growth.

As Paul wrote in his first letter to the church at Corinth,

> *No temptation has seized you except what is common to man. And God is faithful; he will not let you be tempted beyond what you can bear. But when you are tempted, he will also provide a way out so that you can stand up under it* (I Corinthians 10:13).

The exit from such calamity should be marked with a "Grace" sign above the door.

Next, *our weaknesses facilitate God's power*. If you find yourself at the end of your rope, you're in an enviable position, an ideal spot in which God can mold and use you. Divine dominion flourishes in an atmosphere of human weakness.

Jesus' death, burial, and resurrection provide the supreme example of this "power-in-weakness" mystery. The Gospels demonstrates peril giving way to potential. As the Son hung beaten, battered, bruised, and bleeding, eking out His final breath, the Father unleashed a force that shook the earth and split rocks (Matthew 27:51). What took place in the invisible realm was infinitely more significant; sin found permanent atonement, and Satan suffered a crushing defeat. Three days later, that same Power lifted Christ up and out of the grave.

Transformed, Paul sought such power (Philippians 3:10) rather than the fickle and fleeting brand the world had to offer. He prayed that his followers would experience the same (Ephesians 3:16). He dared to boast about his weaknesses and delight in his hardships, fully knowing that Christ's power would take control (II Corinthians 12:9,10).

A. Parnell Bailey visited an orange grove where an irrigation pump had broken down. The season was unusually dry, and some of the trees were beginning to die due to a lack of water. The tour leader then took Bailey to his own orchard, where irrigation had been used sparingly.

> "These trees could go without rain for another two weeks," he said. "You see, when they were young, I frequently kept water from them. This hardship caused

them to send their roots deeper into the soil in search of moisture. Now mine are the deepest-rooted trees in the area. While others are being scorched by the sun, these are finding moisture at a greater depth."[7]

If you find yourself being scorched by stubborn hardship and travail, take delight—thank God for the thorn. He wants you to find "moisture" at a deeper and more meaningful level. You provide the container, and He'll fill you up with living water, which becomes a spring welling up to eternal life—and you'll never thirst again (John 3:14).

---

[1] *www.abcnews.go.com.*

[2] Raymond McHenry, *The Best of In Other Words* (Houston: Raymond McHenry, Publisher, 1996) p. 331.

[3] Eleanor Doan, *Speakers Sourcebook* (Grand Rapids, MI: Ministry Resources Library, 1960) p. 66.

[4] Eleanor Doan, *Speakers Sourcebook II* (Grand Rapids, MI: Ministry Resource Library, 1988) p. 99.

[5] Ibid.

[6] Merrill C. Tenney, General Editor, *The Zondervan Pictorial Encyclopedia of the Bible: Vol. 4* (Grand Rapids, MI: Zondervan Publishing House, 1975) p. 772.

[7] *www.highpraise.com/illustrations.*

1 Peter 4:12-19

Dear friends, do not be surprised at the painful trial you are suffering, as though something strange were happening to you. But rejoice that you participate in the sufferings of Christ, so that you may be overjoyed when his glory is revealed. If you are insulted because of the name of Christ, you are blessed, for the Spirit of glory and of God rests on you. If you suffer, it should not be as a murderer or thief or any other kind of criminal, or even as a meddler. However, if you suffer as a Christian, do not be ashamed, but praise God that you bear that name. For it is time for judgment to begin with the family of God; and if it begins with us, what will the outcome be for those who do not obey the gospel of God? And, "If it is hard for the righteous to be saved, what will become of the ungodly and the sinner?" So then, those who suffer according to God's will should commit themselves to their faithful Creator and continue to do good.

9

Rusty Nails

> *"For it is time for judgment to begin*
> *with the family of God"*
> (I Peter 4:17).

During a courtroom exchange, a defense attorney questioned a farmer with a bodily injury claim. "At the scene of the accident, did you tell the officer you had never felt better in your life?"

"I did," confirmed the farmer.

"Well, then, how is it that you are *now* claiming you suffered serious injury when my client's automobile hit your wagon?"

Leaning forward in his seat, the farmer replied, "When the officer showed up, he went over to my horse Champ, who had a broken leg, and shot him. Then he went over to Rover, my banged-up dog, and shot *him*. When he asked me how *I* felt, I just thought it wise, under the circumstances, to say I've never felt better in my life."

Most of us are guilty of forcing a smile and saying we're doing just fine when, in fact, we could crumble or erupt at any moment. Take, for example, the guy pushing a cart in the supermarket containing, among other things, a screaming baby. Proceeding along the aisles, the man kept repeating softly, "Keep calm, George. Don't get excited, George. Don't yell, George."

A lady watched with admiration and then said, "You are certainly to be commended for your patience in trying to quiet little George."

"Lady," he declared, "*I'm* George!"[1]

We may chuckle at such stories, yet the truth is, many of us give an outward thumbs up when inside our world is in disarray. We trudge up and down the aisles of life, struggling to keep our heads above water, trying to maintain sanity.

The situation was much the same in 63 A.D., the year the apostle Peter wrote his first epistle to believers scattered throughout five different parts of the Roman Empire, all of them in northern Asia Minor (modern Turkey).[2] Under Nero's command, the Romans accelerated their opposition and persecution of the church. Understanding this, Peter penned and sent his letter of hope and encouragement. As we focus on eight verses from chapter four of this brief book, note the following commands concerning tribulation and suffering.

Realize troubles are a part of everyday life, or, as Peter said to his first century readers, "*Do not be surprised at the painful trial you are suffering, as though something strange were happening to you*" (I Peter 4:12). The KJV uses the word *fiery* in the place of *painful*, which symbolizes the connection between tribulation, purification and heat that surfaces regularly throughout the Bible. Job said, "*When he has tested me, I will come forth as gold*" (Job 23:10). "*For you, O God, tested us; you refined us like silver,*" wrote the psalmist (Psalm 66:10).

According to Mildred Witte Struven, "A clay pot sitting in the sun will always be a clay pot. It has to go through the white heat of the furnace to become porcelain."[3] F. B. Meyer, famed English preacher from the late nineteenth and early twentieth centuries, explained this truth as follows:

> A bar of iron worth $2.50, when wrought into horseshoes is worth $5. If made into needles it is worth $175. If made into penknife blades it is worth $1,625. If made into springs for watches it is worth $125,000. What a "trial by fire" that bar must undergo to be worth this! But the more it is manipulated, and the more it is hammered and passed through the heat, beaten, pounded, and polished, the greater its value.[4]

To restate a point made in chapter six, expect storms, rather than being surprised or suppressed by them. And while you're on a roll...

Rejoice in the midst of trials. Do you remember Paul and Silas from two chapters ago? They sang their way through hardship and helped unleash a marvelous series of events. You see, by rejoicing in suffering, you:

Grab the attention of a spiritually needy world. I've watched scores of Larry King interviews over the years, and the best by far was one with Joni Eareckson Tada, who suffered a diving accident and has been a quadriplegic since 1967. Emotion overcame me as Joni rejoiced in her affliction. She said she'd rather be a believer paralyzed in a wheelchair than a healthy lost person with healthy legs and arms. Larry King seemed mesmerized, as I'm sure millions of others were across the world. When hurting people jubilate, people stand up and take notice.

Rejoice in suffering, also, because *you are developing perseverance*. Remember James's challenge to *"consider it pure joy"* when we face difficulties, *"because you know that the testing of your faith develops perseverance"* (James 1:2-3).

A legend exists about an old violin maker who was envied by his colleagues because of the superior quality of the work. One day, he disclosed the secret of his success. While others walked into protected valleys to cut wood for their violins, he climbed the rugged mountain crags for his. There, he discovered just the trees he was looking for—beaten, twisted, and gnarled by the weather. Gale force winds caused their fibers to strengthen and toughen. The storm-tortured heart and grain resulted in an instrument with deep, colorful tones. Likewise, life difficulties fortify the fiber of our heart and soul, creating perseverance that sings.[5]

Next, embrace tribulation because you are in good company, following in worthy footsteps, participating in the sufferings of Christ (see I Peter 4:13). *"For we do not have a high priest who is unable to sympathize with our weaknesses, but we have one who has been tempted in every way, just as we are—yet was without sin"* (Hebrews 4:15). Jesus endured more suffering than any of us will ever experience. Yet we can delight in the misfortune that comes our way, knowing we are identifying with Him. Paul said, *"I want to know Christ...and the fellowship of sharing in his sufferings"* (Philippians 3:10). He understood what would behoove us all to comprehend: crowns come by way of crosses; the blight of this old earth precedes the bliss of the new one.

Finally, we can take pleasure in suffering because *the Helper stands ready to assist,* especially when bearing scorn on behalf of Jesus. As Peter penned, *"If you are insulted because of the name of Christ, you are blessed, for the Spirit of glory...rests on you"* (I Peter 4:14). Just like an angel, or possibly even the pre-incarnate Christ, endured the fiery furnace with Shadrach, Meshach, and Abednego (Daniel 3:23-25), the Holy Spirit who indwells believers provides comfort and protection during difficulty. And while this is certainly worth celebrating, we must also be careful to:

Refrain from unnecessary suffering. I am going to switch from writing into meddling, yet the question must be asked: Are you suffering from something you've brought on yourself? As Peter wrote, *"If you suffer, it should not be as a murderer or thief or any other kind of criminal, or even as a meddler"* (I Peter 4:15). Many of those initially addressed were recent converts, some who came from questionable backgrounds. Peter wants them to understand the difference between agonizing from something over which they had no control versus suffering from their own foolish actions.

Think back to David's debacle discussed in chapter three. He suffered tremendously due to his participation in adultery and murder. There were situations when he praised God in the midst of tribulation, especially those times when his enemies created havoc (Psalm 13). Yet, his affair with Bathsheba merited no rejoicing until he repented and sought forgiveness for it.

Nothing we do can cause God to love us any less. Still, He expects us to avoid attitudes and actions that dishonor Him and cause harm to ourselves in the process.

Next, **recognize** God's judgment in suffering. As Peter stated, *"It is time for judgment to begin with the family of God"* (I Peter 4:17). Solomon said, *"My son, do not despise the* LORD'S *discipline and do not resent his rebuke,* *because the* LORD *disciplines those he loves, as a father the son he delights in"* (Proverbs 3:11-12). Jesus told His disciples the night before the crucifixion that God prunes fruit-bearing branches so that they *"will be even more fruitful"* (John 15:2).

James Michener, one of America's most loved and best-selling novelists, maintained a memory that helped him stay prolific as a writer, well into his old age. When he was five, a neighboring farmer drove eight nails into the trunk of an unproductive apple tree. The following fall, the tired tree yielded a bumper crop of delicious apples. When little James asked how the "miracle" occurred, the farmer replied, "Hammerin' the rusty nails gave it a shock to remind it that its job is to produce apples."[6] Likewise, God leads His children through a jolt now and then to increase our productivity and dependence on Him.

The question is, as Peter so aptly included (I Peter 4:17), if judgment begins with those of us who have received Christ, what about those who reject Him? During this time of extended grace, God allows for more slack in the rope. As Jesus preached in the Sermon on the Mount, *"He causes his sun to rise on the evil and the good, and sends rain on the righteous and the unrighteous"* (Matthew 5:45).

In the grand scheme of things, however, a day of reckoning awaits the unrepentant. They can expect eternity in hell, the second death by way of the lake of fire. If you're not sure of where you stand with Jesus and fear this could be your eventual destination, remember, *"Now is the day of salvation"* (II Corinthians 6:2).

In the midst of the Great Depression, a good man lost his job, depleted his savings, and forfeited his home. On top of all of that, his wife died suddenly, which multiplied his grief. One day, while looking for work, he ran upon stonemasons working on a church building. He noticed in particular one of the men chiselling a triangular piece of rock. Confused about where the piece would fit, he asked, "Where are you going to put that?"

The stonemason pointed to the top of the building and said, "See that little opening up near the spire? That's where it goes. I'm shaping it down here so it will fit in up there."

Recognize God's hand in the struggles you face. He's burning away the dross and chiselling away at the rough edges so you'll flourish down here and fit in up there.

Finally, **recommit** as a result of your suffering. Sadly, many people choose to rebel against or withdraw from God in the midst of misfortune. Peter challenged his readers to do just the opposite: "*Those who suffer according to God's will should commit themselves to their faithful Creator and continue to do good*" (I Peter 4:19).

The original word for *commit* is a banking term that means "to deposit for safekeeping."[7] Upon receiving my paycheck, I take a portion in the form of cash and deposit the remainder in my checking account. I don't drive away from the bank worrying if my money is secure. Likewise, when troubles arise, I must entrust the situation to God and continue to strive toward righteous living.

Consider these examples of the challenge taken from the life of Jeremiah, whom we discussed in chapter four. After his fellow countrymen were captured by force and taken to Babylon, he wrote them a letter, encouraging them to make the best of a bad situation. He instructed them to:

> *Build houses and settle down; plant gardens and eat what they produce. Marry and have sons and*

daughters; find wives for your sons and give your daughters in marriage, so that they too may have sons and daughters. Increase in number there; do not decrease. Also, seek the peace and prosperity of the city to which I have carried you into exile. Pray to the Lord for it, because if it prospers, you too will prosper (Jeremiah 29:5-7).

Jeremiah also assured them that their fortunes would change and they would one day return to their land. He even put his money where his mouth was, purchasing a piece of enemy occupied territory from his cousin Hanamel (Jeremiah 32:8,9). In the end, God rewarded his faith because he practiced what he preached.

A pastor friend of mine told me about a service that took place in his church just prior to the Thanksgiving holiday. People expressed gratitude to God for the things you would expect: salvation, good health, family, etc. Then a lady stood and thanked the Lord for her breast cancer. She told about how the doctor came out after surgery and discussed with her family the diagnosis and treatment. At that point, her unchurched husband suggested that they join hands and pray. It sounds like a simple response, except that she'd never heard him pray before. The husband later became a Christian, and the family is thriving in the church.

If you find yourself residing at wits' end, thank God for it and get ready to grow stronger through the process.

---

[1] Bob Phillips, *The Best of the Good Clean Jokes* (Eugene, OR: Harvest House Publishers, 1989) p. 100.

[2] Warren W. Wiersbe, *Be Hopeful* (Colorado Springs, CO: Chariot Victor Publishing, 1982) p. 11.

3 *www.higherpraise.com.*

4 *www.bible.org.*

5 Richard W. DeHaan and H. G. Bosch, *Our Daily Bread* (Grand Rapids, MI: Daybreak Books, 1959).

6 James A. Michener, *The World is My Home* (New York: Random House, 1992) pp 3-4.

7 Warren W. Wiersbe, *Be Hopeful* (Colorado Springs, CO: Chariot Victor Publishing, 1982) p. 120.

Revelation 5:1-10

Then I saw in the right hand of him who sat on the throne a scroll with writing on both sides and sealed with seven seals. And I saw a mighty angel proclaiming in a loud voice, "Who is worthy to break the seals and open the scroll?" But no one in heaven or on earth or under the earth could open the scroll or even look inside it. I wept and wept because no one was found who was worthy to open the scroll or look inside. Then one of the elders said to me, "Do not weep! See, the Lion of the tribe of Judah, the Root of David, has triumphed. He is able to open the scroll and its seven seals."

Then I saw a Lamb, looking as if it had been slain, standing in the center of the throne, encircled by the four living creatures and the elders. He had seven horns and seven eyes, which are the seven spirits of God sent out into all the earth. He came and took the scroll from the right hand of him who sat on the throne. And when he had taken it, the four living creatures and the twenty-four elders fell down before the Lamb. Each one had a harp and they were holding golden bowls full of incense, which are the prayers of the saints. And they sang a new song: "You are worthy to take the scroll and to open its seals, because you were slain, and with your blood you purchased men for God from every tribe and language and people and nation. You have made them to be a kingdom and priests to serve our God, and they will reign on the earth."

Worthy Is the Lamb

> *"I wept and wept because no one was found who was worthy to open the scroll or look inside"* (Revelation 5:4).

The only survivor of a shipwreck was washed up on a small, uninhabited island. He prayed profusely that God would send someone to rescue him. He searched the horizon every day, yet all he saw was water and sky. Eventually, he built a small hut to protect himself from the elements and to store his meager possessions.

One day, returning from a hunting trip, he discovered his hut in flames. The smoke drifted into the sky as his little house disappeared. Stunned with anger, he cried out, "God, how could you do this to me?" However, the man was awakened the next morning by rescuers. When he asked how they had discovered him, one of them replied, "We saw your smoke signal."

We conclude our journey through the ten major sections of Scripture by examining the words of another who ended up on an island involuntarily and yet discovered, like the man with the burning hut, that problems *do* create opportunities. I'm referring to the apostle John, author of five

New Testament books—the most mysterious being Revelation.

As the first century progressed and the church continued to grow, John became the pastor of the church the apostle Paul started in Ephesus.[1] While serving there, Christians suffered intense persecution under Roman emperor Domitian. As a result, "John was banished to a prison community on Patmos, one of the small Dodecanese islands in the Aegean Sea off the coast of modern Turkey."[2] While living in a cave there and enduring extremely harsh conditions, he received and recorded the apocalyptic imagery reported in Revelation.

In the Spirit on the Lord's day, John caught a look at Christ in heaven: *"His face...like the sun shining in all its brilliance"* (Revelation 1:16). Then, the apostle received another vision of heaven's throne room. Seated in the midst of bizarre creatures and the twenty-four elders (representative of the church triumphant) is God Himself.

As we work our way through this amazing text, note first the **book**, or scroll, as John refers to it. God's *possession* of this divine document in His right hand indicates that history rests firmly in His grasp, no matter how rampant evil may seem or become. He's all-knowing, all-powerful, and all places at all times—always has been and always will be. Nothing catches Him by surprise. Amazingly, such supernal management filters down to the individual level, as King David affirmed, *"If I rise on the wings of the dawn, if I settle on the far side of the sea, even there your hand will guide me, your right hand will hold me fast"* (Psalm 139:9-10).

The fact that the scroll contained writing *on both sides*—a highly unusual practice for that day—indicates the magnitude of the message. This brings to mind one of the dear saints of our church that contacts me now and then. In this era of cell phones, text messaging, e-mail, etc., she actually sends me substantive handwritten letters, using beautiful penmanship, despite her ailing health. On top of that, she has so much good stuff to say that *she writes on both sides of the paper.* God's future plans are so vital and voluminous that it took both sides of the scroll to contain them.

Note, too, that the writing was secured with *seals*, a typical practice in biblical history and beyond. Six centuries before John's Patmos perception, the prophet Daniel received a spectacle of his own. When it concluded, the angel Gabriel said, "*The vision…that has been given you is true, but seal up the vision, for it concerns the distant future*" (Daniel 8:26). After Jeremiah bought the property I mentioned in chapter nine, he "*signed and sealed the deed*" (Jeremiah 32:10).

To the degree that seals were common for those days, the number of them, *seven*, wasn't. Seven signifies completeness. God crafted His creation in six days, then rested on the seventh, an indication of His satisfaction and fulfillment (Genesis 2:2). God told Noah to load the ark with seven pairs of every kind of animal (Genesis 7:2). After the Israelites marched around Jericho for seven days, including seven times on the seventh day, the protective wall collapsed and they captured the city (Joshua 6). Prior to the vision addressed in this chapter, John transcribed letters to the seven churches in the province of Asia.

Obviously, great care was taken in the preparation and protection of this scroll. The tragic flip side is that "*no one in heaven or on earth or under the earth*" was qualified to unwrap its contents (Revelation 5:3). Why? Because, as Robert Mounce explained, "The universe itself was morally incapable of affecting its own destiny."[3] The soiled hands of sinful man wouldn't do when it came to unveiling the future plans of a pure and holy God.

Devastated, John shed **tears**, and one can understand why. He was part of Jesus' inner circle, standing closely by as his Master endured crucifixion (John 19:26). He had served the Lord faithfully for over half a century. And just as God began to unveil His plan for the future, postponement pervaded.

Crying under such circumstances occurs elsewhere in the Bible, revealing a selfless concern for the advancement of God's purpose. While serving as a cupbearer to the Persian king, Nehemiah discovered that the wall around his beloved Jerusalem had been destroyed. Upon receiving the news, he *"sat down and wept"* (Nehemiah 1:4). After mourning, fasting, praying, and receiving permission, he traveled back to the great city to oversee the rebuilding. Five hundred years later, Jesus Himself expressed such emotion as He entered that same place for Passion Week. *"As he approached Jerusalem and saw the city, he wept over it and said, 'If you, even you, had known on this day what would bring you peace—but now it is hidden from your eyes'"* (Luke 19:41-42). So many of His own people failed to recognize Him as Messiah.

Stephen Olford, on hand to assist with counseling and follow-up, recalls a visit to the hotel suite of Billy Graham just days before a 1957 evangelistic crusade in New York City:

> We walked onto the balcony, looking out over the city, and were standing there discussing the crusade, speculating about who would come and how the Lord would work. While we were talking, suddenly I was aware of this big, tall, broad-shouldered man heaving and

breaking down with convulsive weeping. It was almost embarrassing. Billy was crying over the city, like our Lord weeping over Jerusalem.[4]

I once heard an evangelist say that every child of God needed two T's—tears and a testimony. Can you recall a time that you wailed over mankind's sinful state in this lost and dying world? John was crying over God's unrevealed plan when an elder spoke up and said, "*Do not weep!*" (Revelation 5:5). At that point, **One** uniquely qualified—Jesus—stepped forward to open the book.

First, notice His regal *location*, the center of the throne, where creatures and elders gathered around to pay Him just homage. Certainly this suggests His singular sovereignty.

Next, pay particular attention to His diverse *designations*. On the one hand, He is called a Lamb. This description connects to the first Passover, when God rescued Israel from the Egyptians. On that momentous occasion, each Jewish family killed a lamb and spread its blood on the doorpost and lintel of their home. Later, the Lord passed through the land of Egypt and slew the firstborn of every household not sprinkled with blood (Exodus 12). Thus began the sacrifice and feast that became the most important yearly festival in Israel.

Isaiah continued this denotation when predicting Christ's manner of death centuries before it occurred. "*He was led like a lamb to the slaughter, and as a sheep before her shearers is silent, so he did not open his mouth*" (Isaiah 53:7). As that time painfully approached, John the Baptist saw Jesus and said, "*Look, the Lamb of God, who takes away the sin of the world!*" (John 1:29).

Contrasting with this submissive sheep depiction is Christ being called the Lion of the tribe of Judah. This title stems all the way back to Jacob's final blessing on his twelve sons. Here, Judah is called a *"lion's cub"* and is assured that the scepter will not depart from him *"until he comes to whom it belongs"*—Jesus the Messiah (Genesis 49:9-10).

The "Root of David" comes again from Isaiah, who wrote, *"A shoot will come up from the stump of Jesse; from his roots a Branch will bear fruit"* (Isaiah 11:1). Certainly, "Branch" refers to Christ. And at the time of the Lord's birth, the dynasty of David (Jesse's son) fell from towering tree to stump. However, brighter days arrived. From this stump emerged the Spirit-empowered One who lived a sinless life, died, was raised, and then ascended to the right hand of the Father. From such a strategic position, He stepped forth to take the scroll.

Observe, finally, the Lamb's uncommon *characteristics*. *"He had seven horns and seven eyes, which are the seven spirits of God sent out into all the earth"* (Revelation 5:6). This kind of bizarre language steers some away from Revelation, but it shouldn't. A horn signifies strength in the Old Testament, especially in the psalms. David testified, *"The LORD is my rock, my fortress and my deliverer...He is my shield and the **horn** of my salvation"* (Psalm 18:2, emphasis added).

The multiple eyes, also called the spirits of God, indicate total unhindered vision—and on a wider scale, the Lamb's omniscience.

> "In this symbolic way, John pictures the relationship between Christ and the Holy Spirit. In the earlier vision, the symbol of the Spirit—seven torches of fire (Revelation 4:5)—stand before the throne, thus picturing the relationship of the Spirit to God the Father."[5]

And again, as indicated previously, the number seven denotes completeness.

Appropriately, once the suitable candidate came forth to open the scroll, the **music** superseded John's misery. Each elder and creature held a harp and bowl. And while the reason for the instrument seems obvious, the bowls again demonstrate the figurative, often mysterious, nature of this writing. John said these bowls contained incense, *"which are the prayers of the saints"* (Revelation 5:8). Quite likely, these petitions included pleas that God would bring judgment on the wicked and send forth His Kingdom.

Note, in particular, the song, one of many included in Revelation. Like other subjects mentioned in the book—the redeemed, Jerusalem, heaven and earth, and all things—it is described as being new. God specifically composed the song for that moment in history, commemorating a new redeemed order of His Kingdom on the verge of inauguration. Capture the time/eternal totality of the lyrics. The Lamb was worthy because of:

A sacrifice in the past: "*You **were** slain…You **purchased** men for God from every tribe and language and people and nation*" (Revelation 5:9, emphasis added). Christ's death on the cross 2,000 years ago was a once and for all event. "*For God so loved the **world** that he **gave** his one and only Son*" (John 3:16, emphasis added). More specifically, He purchased mankind back from Satan at a price of Jesus' blood. Because of that, we have:

A privilege in the present: If you've trusted in Christ as your Savior, you are a priest. Under the old covenant, priests appeared before God on behalf of the people, serving as mediators. Since the crucifixion, we have direct access to God. And in addition to that, we can look forward to:

A reign in the future: When Christ comes a second time and establishes His Kingdom on the earth, we will reign with Him (Revelation 5:10;20:6). This connects with Jesus' claim that the meek will inherit the earth (Matthew 5:5) and Paul's promise that, "If we endure, we will also reign with him" (II Timothy 2:12). All of these benefits and privileges above—what has been, what is, and what will be—are highlighted in this never-before-sung heavenly verse.

I discovered on the Internet that scores of musically inclined entrepreneurs want to write a special tune just for you. For example, Oregon songwriter Michael Frazier, at a cost of $150, will custom draft a personalized tune for your special event or occasion. He'll even perform it live, if that can be negotiated.[6]

God wants to write you a custom-fit new song, at a cost you could never ever afford—the relinquished life of His only Son. Ironically, you can receive it free, as a gift, if you're willing to relinquish your life to Him. Through the presence of the Holy Spirit, He'll even show up personally to perform it for you. It's all part of what it means to escape wits' end.

---

[1] John MacArthur, *Twelve Ordinary Men* (Nashville: W Publishing Group, 2002) p. 114.

[2] Ibid.

[3] Robert Mounce, *The Book of Revelation: The New International Commentary on the New Testament* (Grand Rapids, MI: William B. Eerdmans Publishing Company, 1977) p. 144.

[4] William A. Martin, *A Prophet with Honor* (New York: William Morrow and Company, 1991) p. 230.

[5] George E. Ladd, *A Commentary on the Revelation of John* (Grand Rapids, MI: William B. Eerdmans Publishing Company, 1972) p. 88.

[6] *www.michaelfrazier.net*.